STAND UP!

From *Farmer-Labor Leader*, January 15, 1930

STAND UP!

The Story
of Minnesota's
Protest Tradition

Rhoda R. Gilman

Minnesota Historical
Society Press

www.mhspress.org

The Minnesota Historical Society Press is a member of the Association of American University Presses.

Manufactured in [the United States of America/Canada]

10 9 8 7 6 5 4 3 2 1

∞ The paper used in this publication meets the minimum requirements of the American National Standard for Information Sciences—Permanence for Printed Library Materials, ANSI Z39.48–1984.

International Standard Book Number
ISBN: 978-0-87351-849-9 (paper)
ISBN: 978-0-87351-857-4 (e-book)

Library of Congress Cataloging-in-Publication Data
Gilman, Rhoda R.
    Stand up! : the story of Minnesota's protest tradition / Rhoda R. Gilman.
        p. cm.
    Includes bibliographical references and index.
    ISBN 978-0-87351-849-9 (paper : alk. paper) — ISBN 978-0-87351-857-4 (e-book)
    1. Protest movements—Minnesota—History. 2. Minnesota—Social conditions. 3. Minnesota—Politics and government 4. Progressivism (United States politics)—History. 5. Social reformers—Minnesota—Biography. 6. Political activists—Minnesota—Biography. 7. Minnesota—Biography. I. Title.
    HN79.M6G55 2012
    322.409776—dc23

                                                                2011040232

Image page 12, Library of Congress.
Photo page 145, Avye Alexandres.
All other images from Minnesota Historical Society collections.

CONTENTS

STAND UP!

INTRODUCTION

*Minnesota is a state spectacularly varied, proud,
and handsome, with a progressive political tradition . . .
It is a state pulled toward East and West both,
and one always eager to turn the world upside down.*

John Gunther, *Inside USA* (1947)

SOME REGARD MINNESOTA'S POLITICAL CULTURE AS MORAL-
istic and some see it as radical, but most would agree that it
has been a seedbed for cultural and political movements that
have changed the country, and its history weaves a pattern
of wide opposition between left and right. This tension may
account for the frequent presence of alternative parties and
electoral experiments. As a historian and political activist, I
have often been asked such questions as: "Why are Minnesota Democrats called the DFL?"—"Have we always had third
parties?"—and "Who was Ignatius Donnelly?—Floyd Olson?—

1

Gus Hall?" Yet there has been no brief, readable work that would summarize the story and answer those factual questions. After working for many years as a Minnesota historian and taking part in struggles for social change during my own times, I have tried here to provide one.

This is a story of successive protest movements, including political parties and other organizations that have sought to gain power within the state and to shape its government along with its social and economic patterns. It is a story of conflict and defeat, of change and tenacity. I have tried to give enough of the historical framework to make the context clear and the movements understandable, but I have left interpretation and analysis to deeper and more detailed studies. There are plenty of those. Some are listed in the bibliography at the end of the book.

Power in American society is about wealth, so the root of most protest has been economic. Nevertheless, there have been demands for racial, religious, ethnic, or gender rights, and those have sometimes divided or derailed movements that were formed along lines of economic power. Protest can be conservative as well as radical, and if "radicalism" is defined as rapid change at the roots, then many of Minnesota's protest movements have been conservative in the sense of struggling to preserve the local control and small-scale business of an agrarian society against the steady march of corporate industry and the concentration of wealth.

Movements based on single issues, such as prohibition or abortion, have enlisted strong passions and have raised serious questions about the fairness of the American two-party system and its electoral laws. More broadly based small parties have challenged those laws with proposals to replace plurality ("winner take all") voting with a system based on ranked choice. With its persistent small-party tradition, it is no wonder that Minnesota has been in the forefront of that effort.

An exception to the usual pattern of protest has been the long and continuing fight to secure equality for women. This fight has coincided almost exactly with the existence of Minnesota as a territory and state, but it is far wider than just giving votes and political office to women. Like the struggle to save the earth's environment, which has only begun, the empowerment of women affects customs and religious beliefs that have endured through many generations of human society. Ecofeminists see a profound relationship between the status of women and that of the earth. As we look ahead, the preservation of the planet's living systems seems certain to demand fundamental changes not only in our politics but in the values that underlie our industrial civilization. One such change is likely to be the increased importance of a local economy and hence of local government. So the story of Minnesota's protest heritage may be more significant to readers in the next century than in the last one.

As the timeline of history merges into the present, the landscape flattens and it is hard to know which peaks and valleys will stand out as we move beyond them. At the same time, it can be instructive for a historian to come off her perch as an observer and to take responsibility for her place as an actor. My involvement with the Green Party has made me part of the developments discussed in the last chapters. But journalists are not the only ones who write the first drafts of history, and I describe Minnesota's recent protest movements in order to place them firmly in the context of the state's protest tradition—and to draw lessons about their meaning.

1. "THE ACRES AND THE HANDS"

MINNESOTA POLITICS BEGAN WHEN THE TERRITORY WAS OR-
ganized. The year was 1849. The United States had just invaded Mexico and taken the northern third of the country, including California. The gold rush there was in full swing. But the
real gold of the great West was, and always had been, its land.

The forests and prairies and mountains were sacred to Indian people, but in a very different way they were also sacred
to the hoards of squatters and sodbusters who were ready to
take them and turn them into ranches and farms and towns.
The convictions of those eager immigrants were captured in a
set of verses printed in one of St. Paul's first newspapers:

> Sunlight and music, and gladsome flower,
> Are over the earth spread wide;
> And the good God gave those gifts to men—
> To men who on earth abide.
> Yet thousands are toiling in poisonous gloom,
> And shackled with iron bands,

Yet millions of hands want acres,
And millions of acres want hands.
'Tis writ that "ye shall not muzzle the ox,
That treadeth out the corn."
Yet behold ye shackle the poor man's hand
That have all earth's burdens borne;
The land is the gift of bounteous God,
And to labor his word commands;
Yet millions of hands want acres,
And millions of acres want hands.
Who hath ordained that few should hoard
Their millions of useless gold,
And rob the earth of its fruits and flowers,
While profitless soil they hold?
Who hath ordained that the parchment scroll
Should fence round miles of land,
While millions of hands want acres,
And millions of acres want hands?

By 1849 the direction of U.S. policy toward the vast stretches of land taken from Native Americans had already been threshed out. Conservative investors in the eastern states, mainly represented by the Whig Party, argued that western land should be sold at the highest price it would bring. The money would be used to pay the national debt and run the government, and any left over could be divided among the states. This raised a storm of protest from immigrants, workers, and western farmers, who were united behind the Democratic Party and their champion, President Andrew Jackson. The land was there to be used, they said. The more it was settled and cultivated, the faster America would grow. Give it away to the people, and let them build the country!

An even stronger argument was the impossibility of preventing people from taking the land. Whether it belonged to Indian tribes or to the government, whether it was surveyed or not, the squatter moved in, cleared a field, and built his shanty. Then he and his neighbors united to fight anyone who tried to move them out, whether by force or by law. And no politician wanted to be in the nasty position of ordering American settlers driven from their homes.

So Indians were ruthlessly forced or tricked into signing treaties that gave up their land to the government, and most were deported, or "removed" westward beyond the line of white settlement. As years passed, the price of public land was lowered, smaller pieces were offered for sale, land offices were opened in places where settlers could reach them easily, land was sold on credit, and finally in 1841 a general preemption act was passed to take the place of temporary laws enacted earlier.

Under the 1841 law settlers could register a claim on any piece of surveyed government land, live on it, improve it, and have first chance to "prove up" or pay for it before the government declared the area open for sale at auction. Even this did not satisfy the people of frontiers like Minnesota. Not many settlers had the cash to pay for their claims, and they lived in fear that their small homesteads would be bought by speculators with large pockets. So they put pressure on their representatives to have the government delay land sales and allow settlers to continue farming freely on public land. In the background was always the hope that Congress would someday pass a homestead act and give the land to anyone willing to live on it.

As a last resort, settlers in an area faced with a land sale would form a "claim association" to prevent anyone from bidding against them at the auction. One such association in Minnesota distributed a proclamation that read,

> RESOLVED THAT: Wee, united to a man, does now and hereafter stand boldly up and defend our mutual interests and wrights against any and all aggressions wich may be made upon us.

> RESOLVED THAT: While wee are firm and unwavering advocates and upholders of the Law, yet doe wee not recognise or abide by the justice wich to often obtains in its administrasion that might and wealth make wright, and wee tharefore in this instence appeal to the higher law of justice and wright—the Law of equel and exact Justice between Man and Man, not more, not less—and wich wee will have, then let The Hevens Fall.

> RESOLVED THAT: Wee repair to the Land Sales en masse to protect . . . from the bids of wealthy and sordid speculators . . . the homes wich shelter our wives and little ones.

In 1848, a year before Minnesota became a territory, a land sale was scheduled that included the small settlement of St. Paul. Many of those who had not "proved up" the land on which their houses and shops stood were French Canadians with little command of English. They formed an association and asked Henry H. Sibley, the leading Minnesota businessman, to go to the sale and bid on their property. Nearly all of them had dealt with Sibley for years, and they trusted him. Sibley, on his part, had political ambitions, and he quickly agreed to help. Accompanied by a crowd armed with heavy clubs, he went to the auction at St. Croix Falls and bought for the settlers at the minimum government price the land they had claimed in what is now St. Paul. Everyone agreed that it would have taken a brave man to bid against him.

*　*　*

When a territory was created, the president appointed all of its officers and judges; the people could elect a legislature and a representative (who had no vote) to Congress. In 1849 President Zachary Taylor, a Whig, gave the offices in the new territory to members of his own party. Sibley, like nearly everyone else in Minnesota, was a Democrat. He was elected to Congress, and the new Whig governor, Alexander Ramsey, was faced with a legislature that was nearly all Democratic. Ramsey was above all else a practical man, so he quickly made friends with Sibley, and the two developed a bipartisan working relationship. The only opposition was from a splinter group of Democrats led by Sibley's rival, Henry M. Rice.

Land was, of course, the top priority. All of Minnesota west of the Mississippi River was owned by Indian tribes—but not for long. In the next six years, most of southern Minnesota and the territory between the head of Lake Superior and the source of the Mississippi were taken by treaties forced upon the Dakota and Ojibwe. The agreements were grossly unfair, but the older chiefs knew only too well that if they did not sign, the land would be taken anyway and they would be driven out. So they made the best bargains they could. The younger men and traditional religious leaders were fiercely opposed to the sale.

The most important of the treaties were two signed in 1851 by which the four bands of Dakota Indians gave up their homeland in southern Minnesota. Henry Sibley, who had been the principal trader with the tribe for nearly twenty years, played a key role in the negotiations; then, as representative for the territory in Washington, he had the job of persuading Congress to pay for the land. Sibley himself had a financial interest in the process, since he had lost money in the trading business and owed debts that could be repaid only with

Indian treaty money. Both his political future and his personal solvency were at stake.

He succeeded, but at a terrible cost. The treaties, which cheated the Dakota and confined them to a narrow, inadequate reservation along the Minnesota River, set the stage for the war that broke out in 1862. Sibley, a proud and sensitive man with friends and family ties among the Dakota, rarely spoke of the treaties after they had been approved. He preferred to forget them. Ramsey, who shared the responsibility, was more blunt in boasting of the bargain they had secured for the country.

In fact, neither man could have changed the course of American empire. As soon as word spread that the Dakota had agreed to sell, and long before the treaties had been amended and ratified, the dam burst. Illegal settlers poured across the Mississippi, staking out farms and platting towns on land that had not been surveyed and still belonged to the Dakota. As Sibley lobbied feverishly in Washington, Ramsey wrote to him, complaining about the delay. "We have grown quite familiar," the governor said, "with the names of some half dozen embryo towns on that side [of the Mississippi]." Sibley admitted that now the land could never be returned to the Indians, but he feared that if the treaty failed, war would break out. His fear was justified. Although the war was delayed for ten years, it came in 1862 and was the most tragic episode in the state's history.

The attack began as a complete surprise on an August morning in 1862, and within two or three days more than five hundred white civilians had been slain. The attack was launched by an extremist faction of the tribe—mostly young men—who were reluctantly joined by Chief Little Crow. To a majority of the Dakota it was as much a shock as to their white neighbors. Nevertheless, the panic and hysteria it pro-

duced led to cries for revenge on all Indians. After a short conflict, some Dakota fled to the western plains and to Canada.
Thirty-eight were convicted of murder and hanged, and the
rest, along with the unoffending Winnebago, were deported,
eventually to Nebraska. Along the way an uncounted number
of Dakota women and children died of starvation and disease,
while sporadic warfare continued on the plains for another
generation.

For European Americans the Dakota War removed the last
barrier to settlement of western Minnesota. Although the
Homestead Act, which had been passed in the spring of 1862,
was already in effect, the rich reservation land in the Minnesota Valley taken from the Dakota and Winnebago was not
opened to homesteaders but was sold at government auction.
Some of it had already been broken and cultivated by Indian
farmers, and scarcely any immigrant settlers had the cash to
buy it. Most of it went to wealthy speculators.

Long before the Homestead Act, an even greater giveaway of
government land was under way. The railroad age had begun,
and in 1854 the first train reached the Mississippi River at
Rock Island. But already in 1850 the Illinois Central had received a huge grant of government land to stimulate building
its line, and within a year there was a mad scramble among
eastern railroad promoters, western land investors, and the
politicians who represented them to secure more.

Railroad land grants were not at first given directly to private companies but to the states or territories. Those governments then passed them on to railroads chartered within
their boundaries. The usual plan gave the railroad alternate
sections of land for a specified distance on each side of the
right of way. In theory this would allow railroads to be built

American Progress, an 1872 painting by Prussian American painter John Gast, was commissioned by a publisher of western travel guides. It captures the idea of Manifest Destiny: that the United States was destined to expand across North America.

into regions that were not yet settled. The company would recover some of its investment by selling land to settlers, who would then within a few years provide business for its line. Meanwhile the sections of land still held by the government would be increased in value by the fact that transportation was available. Like present-day tax increment financing (TIF), it promised to be a win-win deal.

In spite of this, popular support for railroad land grants was never unanimous. Many of those dedicated to the idea of free land for the landless felt that the increased price to be charged for both railroad and government land was a disguised tax upon the people to subsidize railroads. Others saw dangers of monopoly and political favoritism in giving control over so much of a state's land to a private corporation.

But in Minnesota as elsewhere, these misgivings were drowned out in the clamor for "progress." The country was dazzled by the prospects and promises of a railroad era, with tracks stretching from coast to coast. Editors, promoters, and politicians urged the need to build them at any cost, and even from the pulpit people were told that the steam whistle echoed the voice of God. On June 11, 1854, one of St. Paul's leading ministers, the Reverend Edward D. Neill, preached a sermon on "Railways in Their Higher Aspects," taking his text from the prophet Isaiah: "The voice of him that crieth in the wilderness, Prepare ye the way of the Lord, make straight in the desert a highway for our God."

Just eighteen days after Neill preached his sermon, the president signed into law a railroad land grant for Minnesota. It was the first given to any territory. The fate of that grant, which was quickly revoked, foreshadowed the long and dismal story of corruption and financial influence that surrounded the politics of railroad land grants, both in Minnesota and in the whole nation.

The bill in question called for a grant of land to Minnesota to build a railroad from the head of Lake Superior by way of St. Paul to connect with the line of the Illinois Central Railway at Dubuque, Iowa. Political and financial support for the measure came from the powerful interests that backed the Illinois Central. A company known as the Minnesota and North Western Railroad was organized to receive the grant. Its incorporators were representatives of the Illinois Central and a number of influential Minnesotans, most of them friends of Henry Rice, who had succeeded Sibley in 1853 as the territory's congressional delegate. Rice had large landholdings at

Superior, Wisconsin, which would skyrocket in value with the building of a railroad.

Sibley also supported the idea of the land grant bill, but he and his political friends, both in Minnesota and in Congress, objected to the coziness of the arrangement with Rice and the Illinois Central. When Congress refused to pass it, Sibley drafted a bill that gave the land to a newly formed company and not to one that was already closely held. Congress agreed, but at some time after the new bill was passed its wording was secretly altered to give the land back to the Minnesota and North Western. In other states the financiers behind the Illinois Central had bullied or bribed politicians to go along with similar tactics, but Sibley was a different breed. He blew the whistle. Congress immediately repealed the act, and railroad building in Minnesota was delayed for nearly a decade.

New land grants were made, however, in 1857 and throughout the 1860s. Eventually grants to railroads accounted for more than 18 percent, or nearly a fifth, of Minnesota's total area. Only in North Dakota and Washington State did railroads take a larger proportionate bite of the public lands. The greatest single grant went to the Northern Pacific Railroad, which got well over a million acres in Minnesota alone. Soon the cheering stopped, and before many years had passed the public enthusiasm for railroads had turned to bitterness, especially among pioneer farmers.

2. "THE ABOLITION WAGON"

THE MOST BITTER AND VIOLENT CRISIS OF MINNESOTA POLItics occurred just as the territory was becoming a state. The passions that tore apart the nation over slavery blew through the upper Mississippi country like a tornado, dividing neighbors, rearranging party lines, and threatening the hopes for statehood. Although for the majority of citizens the real issue was preserving the nation, Minnesota had ardent abolitionists, and there were also furious defenders of slavery. One of the defenders was the editor of the *Chatfield Democrat*, who printed some jeering verses about those who jumped on the wagon of freedom:

> *Come all treacherous Abolitionists,*
> *and join in hostile band,*
> *You're going to invade the Southern men*
> *and drive them from their land.*
> *Disunion is your motto, and satan is your guide,*
> *So jump into the wagon, and all take a ride.*

Wait for the wagon,
The Abolition wagon;
The Negro's in the wagon,
And you'll all take a ride.
Your cause is most unholy, you are disloyal too.
To smash the Constitution
is what you want to do;
With success to crown your efforts,
and satan for your guide,
Jump into the wagon and to Tophet take a ride.
Come hurry up the wagon,
The Abolition wagon,
Disunion is your wagon,
And you'll all take a ride.

Legally, Minnesota had been free territory since 1787. Yet slavery did exist there. The best-known case is that of Dred Scott, a black man owned by one of the officers at Fort Snelling. Scott was taken back to the slave state of Missouri and later sued for his freedom, but it was denied by the U.S. Supreme Court. There were many others not so famous.

During the 1820s and '30s, nearly all the commissioned officers at the fort either owned household slaves or rented their services from others who did. Part of an army officer's pay was a stipend for a personal servant, and few white people were willing to hire out as servants at a remote frontier post. Many officers were from the South, so they either brought along or acquired slaves. The Mississippi River was a broad highway leading directly to the South and its slave markets. The army simply looked the other way, and since the army was the only law in frontier areas, slavery was widely practiced. Even a few local traders and farmers kept slaves.

Dred Scott

By the 1840s times were changing. Church missionaries were arriving, hoping to convert the Indians to Christianity, and many of them had moral objections to slavery. Tribal land on the east bank of the Mississippi had been sold, and lumbermen were coming from New England to cut themselves a fortune in "the pineries." They, too, had doubts about slavery, and a few had been influenced by the radical abolition movement in the northeastern states. So by 1849, when Minnesota Territory was organized, opposition to slavery had grown, local courts were ready to enforce the law, and for the most part slavery was politically a nonissue.

* * *

All of that changed again in the mid-1850s with passage of the Kansas-Nebraska Act, which opened the western territories to slavery if local people voted for it, and with the U.S. Supreme Court's decision in the case of Dred Scott, which defined slaves even in free states and territories as property like any other commodity. In 1857, the year of the Dred Scott decision, Minnesota stood on the threshold of statehood. Its booming lumber industry was still drawing people from the Northeast, and immigrants were pouring in from Europe—Germans, Scandinavians, and Irish, who had no experience with slavery and wanted none. They looked to the day when the vast plains of the West would be opened to small homesteads, and they had no wish to see the land taken up with large plantations worked by black slaves.

The Whig Party had never really existed in Minnesota, and it collapsed throughout the country in 1852 because it refused to take a stand on the simmering questions over slavery. The Democratic Party was divided, but its leaders were southern slaveholders, and they hung on to power in Congress and the White House. In Minnesota, Henry Rice spoke for the proslavery Democrats, which included the governor and all territorial officeholders appointed by the president. Henry Sibley led the centrist antislavery wing.

There was clearly a need for a new party to represent the growing number of people who were sickened by the threat of slavery spreading across the continent and by the law that forced them to return runaway slaves to their owners. By 1854 men throughout the northwestern states were getting together to talk about the question. They were a miscellaneous lot. Some had been Whigs, some were moderate antislavery Democrats, and some were Free Soilers, who had left the Democratic Party in 1848. A few were prohibitionists (then known as "temperance" folk), and a few were associated with the Know-Nothings, a semisecret movement that preached distrust of foreigners and Catholics. Meetings that soon adopted the name "Republican" were held that year in Ohio, Indiana, Illinois, Michigan, Wisconsin, and Iowa.

One such meeting was also held at the tiny village of St. Anthony Falls in Minnesota. The two men who organized it were both New Englanders with extreme views. John W. North, who later founded the town of Northfield, was a visionary abolitionist and friend of William Lloyd Garrison and Frederick Douglass. The Reverend Charles Gordon Ames was a Unitarian minister and an ardent enemy of alcohol.

The Minnesota Republican movement had broadened by the time its first convention was held nine months later, but the echo of hymns and the rumble of the Underground Railroad could still be heard when Ames declared that there was a "natural affinity between the friends of Prohibitory Law, the friends of Civil Liberty and the friends of political reform." Those at the convention agreed unanimously.

Republican leaders wasted no time in calling another convention to write a platform and choose a candidate for the territory's delegate to Congress. There was no question about whom they wanted to run; the leading non-Democrat in Minnesota was Alexander Ramsey, the former territorial governor. But Ramsey was decidedly cool to the new party. He maintained that he was still a Whig, not a Republican, and he absolutely refused to be nominated. A cautious, shrewd man, Ramsey had little in common with ideological fire-eaters like Ames and North. He played a waiting game on the question of slavery, and he was known for having a friendly beer now and then with German voters.

The platform of Minnesota Republicans in 1855 called for

both abolition and prohibition. It was a mistake. German and Irish immigrants could see no "natural affinity" whatever between freeing blacks and forbidding whites to drink what they chose. There were other things also that put them off. Anti-Catholic and antiforeign paranoia occasionally crept into Republican statements. That summer a Republican caucus near Hastings adopted a resolution against "ecclesiastical slavery, which enchains the minds of masses of men, . . . so as to make them move or fight, or vote at the dictation of a princely hierarchy that assumes to be 'the church.'" The same party meeting condemned "foreigners banding themselves together in separate organizations as Irish or Germans, and thus keeping up their old nationalities, when it should rather be their endeavor to become Americanized."

Therefore many of the territory's foreign born turned their backs on the Republicans and voted instead for David Olmsted, who ran as an independent, antislavery Democrat. This split aided the reelection of the regular Democrat, Henry Rice, who had already served one term. Rice was an influential and popular businessman. He had no strong personal feelings about slavery, but he appreciated a glass of good Kentucky bourbon and he valued the power that his friendships with leading southern politicians gave him in Washington.

The flames of the slavery issue could not be smothered for long, however. In Kansas, where the question of slavery in the future state was left to a popular vote, open warfare broke out. As reports of wholesale murders and pitched battles came from "Bleeding Kansas," even cautious and practical men were stirred and alarmed. In 1856 the Republican Party held its first national convention, and this time Alexander Ramsey not only attended but helped to write the platform.

Minnesota was not threatened with warfare over slavery, but the same bitterness that tore Kansas apart almost torpedoed the sober work of framing a state constitution. To those for whom ending human slavery or preserving the destiny of the nation were burning moral issues, the question of which party would control the new state became more important than the future of Minnesota itself.

As the election of delegates to the constitutional convention drew near in 1857, the debate between Democrats and Republicans centered on allowing black suffrage. The votes of the handful of free blacks who lived in Minnesota was not the question; the real issue was the social and political status of black people. When freed from slavery, were they to be accepted as human beings with the same inalienable rights called for by the Declaration of Independence? Minnesota Democrats played on the fears of white people and made it a key issue in their campaign. "WHITE SUPREMACY AGAINST NEGRO EQUALITY!" screamed a headline in the *St. Paul Pioneer and Democrat* only days before the election.

The vote was evenly divided, and there were contested delegates. Feelings were so intense that neither party would trust the other to run the convention. The result was a two-ring circus: Republicans and Democrats meeting separately at opposite ends of the capitol and drawing up two constitutions. The Democrats had an edge because on the whole they were older and more experienced at government. Although the delegates of the parties worked separately, they stayed at the same hotels, shared drinks at the same bars, and often compared notes. As the days went by it became clear that, except for certain key issues, the two documents were not that different. At last Senator Stephen A. Douglas, a national leader of the antislavery Democrats, paid a visit to St. Paul and persuaded the Minnesota Democrats that failing to compromise on a single constitution would be fatal.

So the two sides agreed on a small committee to work out the remaining differences. Even that effort nearly blew apart when Willis Gorman, a former territorial governor who was noted for a hot temper, broke his cane over the head of a Republican who he thought had said something insulting. Nevertheless, they reached the critical compromise over suffrage by barring blacks from voting but making the new constitution easily amended by a simple majority of the people. Eleven years later, in 1868, after four years of bloody warfare and passage of the Thirteenth and Fourteenth Amendments to the U.S. Constitution, Minnesota at last gave the vote to its black male citizens.

Agreement on a state constitution did not mean immediate statehood. Enmity in Congress was so deep that it could function only if the existing balance between slave and free states was maintained. Minnesota's admission was delayed for nearly eight months, until slaveholders won the war in Kansas and it was accepted as a slave state. Meanwhile, Minnesota had held its first state elections in the fall of 1857. There were accusations of fraud on both sides, but the Democrats won by a paper-thin margin, electing Henry Sibley as governor.

Many fiery speeches were given in the course of the constitutional convention, but what may have been the wisest words were spoken by a little-known delegate named Oscar Perkins, an abolitionist from Rice County, who called for political leadership: "The people," he said, referring to the voters, "are not prepared for equal suffrage, and I apprehend if they are not prepared for it at this time, they never will be prepared, unless those who assume to be the leaders of the multitude prepare them. Somebody has to take the step in advance."

One step in advance was taken two years later, in 1859, when Republicans swept the new state, electing Ramsey governor and assuring that Abraham Lincoln would take Minnesota in the presidential election of 1860. Ramsey's running mate for the office of lieutenant governor was a young newcomer named Ignatius Donnelly. Addressing his fellow Irish Americans, he gave a ringing new tone to Republican rhetoric:

> Can the foreign-born voter, fleeing from oppression in the old lands of Europe, hesitate in his choice? He came here to share our liberty—will he take sides with the Cause of Bondage? He left the old world to escape the injustice of a moneyed aristocracy—will he aid to build up another in the new? He came to find the land where labor stood on an equality with wealth; will he assist to make labor synonymous with degredation and lifelong servitude?

The Democrats, beaten for the first time since 1849, tried desperately to pull themselves together. Most Minnesota Democrats were actually against slavery. Like other northern Democrats, they clung to their party because they saw it as the last and only hope of keeping the country together and avoiding the nightmare of civil war. But the hold of the Democratic Party on the loyalty of the state's frontier settlers was broken, and it would be forty years before Minnesota elected another Democratic governor.

3. GRANGERS AND GREENBACKS

IN THE POST–CIVIL WAR YEARS, MINNESOTANS SAW AND participated in the taking of the northern plains from Indian people, the final slaughter of the wild buffalo herds, and the end of the western frontier within a single generation. Meanwhile, the agrarian West was being swamped by the explosive growth of an urban industrial economy. In 1872 a direct railroad connection was opened between St. Paul and Chicago, and in 1883 Minnesota celebrated the completion of a transcontinental line to the north Pacific coast. Just as steel tracks knit the country together physically, a new system of nationally chartered and regulated banks knit it together financially and gave it a standard currency. Corporations, made commonplace by the railroads, became the usual form of business organization, and in 1886 a corporation was declared by the courts to be an artificial person with all the rights of a natural one. Among those rights was owning the shares of other corporations, so pyramids of centralized money and power could easily be built.

Politically, Minnesota was dominated by the Republican Party, although the Democrats hung on to pockets of power, especially in St. Paul, St. Cloud, and other communities where the immigrant and Catholic vote was strong. Alexander Ramsey, who by then was known to political insiders as "the Old Coon," was the unquestioned leader of Minnesota Republicans until 1875. What had been the upstart antislavery party of the 1850s weeded out young radicals like Ignatius Donnelly and became the voice of aging and conservative Civil War veterans, who were organized in the Grand Army of the Republic (GAR). Very few issues divided the two parties during these years. Everyone was for "progress."

But progress for whom? It soon became an uncomfortable question that neither party was willing to ask. Enriched by land grants, railroads quickly combined into large networks owned by those with access to eastern banks. Their monopoly advantage over thousands of small farmers was immediately reflected in higher rates for storing and shipping crops. No one had waited for the coming of the iron rails more eagerly than the frontier farmer, and no one supported more enthusiastically the great gifts of public land that made railroad building profitable. Yet when the train at last steamed along the tracks, the farmer often felt that it had come to run him down.

The heavy, brutal work of turning the wild prairies with their tall grass and thick sod into farms made men old before their time. Repeated cash crops of corn and wheat wore out the rich soil, and every penny left over from feeding a family went to building fences and barns, buying expensive machinery, and paying for livestock. Isolated on scattered farms far from neighbors and relatives and raising children in sod huts or log cabins, women suffered even more.

* * *

One Minnesota man thought he had an answer. Oliver H. Kelley owned a farm near Elk River, but he was a better promoter and journalist than a farmer. He claimed to be "as full of public spirit as a dog is full of fleas." An energetic member of the Masonic Lodge, Kelley thought that a brotherhood of farmers based on principles and ideals like those of Freemasonry might foster dignity and mutual help. So in 1868 he started an organization called the Patrons of Husbandry. Local chapters were known as Granges, and the shorter name was soon used informally for the whole organization. The idea spread like wildfire, not only in Minnesota but in neighboring states and soon to the whole country.

Perhaps because Kelley shared his dreams and his organizing work with his niece, Caroline Hall, the Grange was open to women, with certain symbolic offices reserved for them. Thus it became a family organization, and Grange picnics, held in the summer by each chapter, became the great social event of the season in many farm communities. Gathered together, men and women talked over their problems. Skills and information were shared; buying clubs and cooperatives were formed; friendships were made, and leaders emerged. As Kelley had hoped, energy and self-respect grew stronger. So did anger and a sense of injustice.

The early 1870s brought even greater hardships for frontier farmers. Grasshoppers came in devastating clouds that destroyed crops throughout western Minnesota. Then in 1873 a financial panic spread depression across the country. It was still a world without such things as social security, crop and unemployment insurance, disaster loans, or an organized welfare system. The state provided some relief funds, and more were collected from private charity, but it was far too little. One Becker County man was among hundreds of desperate farmers who wrote to the governor asking for help.

A cartoon by W. E. S. Trowbridge of the 1870s, "The Irrepressible Conflict"

I Olen J—with Wife and Six Children the Oldest about ten years Came to the Country four years ago; poor; the grashoppers has destroid the crope more or lase every year but one. I got along very well as long as I could get planty woork, but sence this Money Cre[sis] cam on, and the woork stoped, it is no plase were a man can mak a cent.

A woman from near Alexandria wrote, "We have not bought any clothing since we came here, for it has took all we could raise to live, without buying clothes. My husband has not had a sock on his feet this winter, and he suffers very much with the cold."

After a few grim years, the grasshoppers left, but the poverty and depression stayed on. Crop prices kept falling, while mortgage payments and railroad rates and the cost of farm machinery remained the same. The farmers' anger turned first toward the railroads. Crops were worthless unless they could be shipped to market.

As early as December 1870, an antimonopoly convention was held in Rochester and a proclamation was issued that detailed the "gross outrages" to which farmers of the first congressional district were subjected by the Winona and St. Peter Railroad Company. It not only charged high rates but gave discounts and rebates to favored customers, and, through ownership of the grain storage elevators along its line, it held the sole power to set the grades of the grain that farmers offered for sale. In January another antimonopoly meeting was held in St. Paul, and in response the Minnesota legislature of 1871 passed a law limiting railroad rates and forbidding the lines from discriminating among customers. The railroads claimed that such regulation was unconstitutional and refused to obey it.

A leader at the St. Paul convention was former lieutenant governor and congressman Ignatius Donnelly, one of Minnesota's most popular lecturers. Soon he agreed to speak at Grange meetings around the state on vital issues of the day. His words to the farmers were blunt and to the point:

> In 1860 it cost *nineteen cents* to carry a bushel of wheat from Chicago to New York. In 1873 it costs *thirty-seven cents—nearly double!*
> Why? There are now more railroads to carry the produce and more produce to be carried than in 1860. The reason is *there is more robbery.*

So enthusiastically was Donnelly's message received among farmers that within a year the number of local Granges had grown from fifty to more than three hundred. When farmers listened to him and talked with each other, they realized that in unity and organization lay power. Donnelly urged them on: "If you agree with fifty men around you as to the next world, you come together and form a church; if you agree with fifty men around you as to this world, you come together and form a party . . . Why all your agitation, discussion, meetings, resolutions, if you do not take hold of the ballot box?"

When some shook their heads and argued that the aims of the Grange were social and that its constitution forbade it from getting into politics, Donnelly retorted, "Why make a gun that will do everything but shoot?"

So in 1873 the Grangers organized an Anti-Monopoly Party in Minnesota, and in coalition with the Democrats it controlled the legislature of 1874. Republicans read the signs of the times, and they repudiated the entrenched leadership of Ramsey to nominate for governor a young lawyer named Cushman K. Davis, who had lectured across the state on the evils of large corporations.

As in Illinois, Iowa, Wisconsin, and Missouri, Grangers in Minnesota succeeded in passing another strong law to regulate railroads. But the northeastern and southwestern parts of the state did not yet have railroad service, and people there were more anxious to encourage than to restrain the corporations. Therefore the law was quickly watered down, and for a few years the frustration of the farmers turned in other directions.

The Panic of 1873 was followed by nearly a decade of falling prices and business stagnation. This depression was aggravated by the government's policy of calling in the "greenbacks," or paper currency, that had been issued by the U.S. Treasury during the Civil War and putting the country back on the gold standard. This favored the banks and eastern financial institutions at the expense of debtors, and nearly all midwestern farmers were in debt. New settlers, many of them immigrants, had no capital except their own labor. Some of them were able to borrow money for making improvements by mortgaging their land, but interest rates were high. While fortunes were made by millers, timber owners, and railroad financiers, farmers found that the harder they worked, the less they earned. So they next attacked the financiers, the currency system, the tax and tariff laws, and the high interest rates that seemed to be grinding them into the ground.

In the mid-1870s the Minnesota Anti-Monopoly Party changed its name to Anti-Monopoly Independent, and by the presidential election of 1876 it was fully identified with the national Greenback Labor Party, which advocated currency managed by the government and not tied to the value of gold. Although party speakers and writers engaged in many long discussions of the monetary question, it remained a complicated subject and difficult for most people to understand. So campaigning often came down to class-conscious slogans and rousing songs with economics as bad as their poetry. The party's newspaper, the *Anti-Monopolist,* sang about the virtues of abandoning the two-party system:

> All hail the National Greenback cause!
> Let every free man break
> And cast away his party chains
> For his salvation's sake.
> In God we trust; our cause is just,
> And may our country be
> From interest, mortgage, bonds and debts
> Forever soon set free.

In 1878 Minnesota's Democratic Party again joined with the Independents, and both groups nominated Ignatius Donnelly for congressman from the state's third district, which then included the city of Minneapolis and most of west-central Minnesota. His opponent, the Republican candidate, was William D. Washburn, a member of a wealthy Minneapolis milling family. Although Donnelly supported the Greenback cause, he concentrated his campaign on an issue much closer to the hearts of wheat farmers in the western counties.

With the growth of flour mills in Minneapolis, the power over grading and pricing of Minnesota wheat had come to rest in the hands of a few large milling companies, and once more the farmers saw themselves as exploited victims of a great monopoly. In what became known as "the brass kettle campaign," Donnelly, who was one of the state's best orators, gave voice to their feelings:

> The farmers have discovered that there is a gigantic conspiracy to rob them of the fruits of their industry—a ring of millers, who by their swindling brass kettles [wheat testers] are determined to reduce the quality and the price of wheat . . . A farmers' meeting at Minneapolis tried the tester with the sealed half bushel, and in every case the result was that the tester weighed less . . . The wheat is graded down by this infamous swindle.
>
> [Washburn] replies that he is not one of the ring, and he is not a miller, but he was and is a member of a milling firm, and takes his share of the stealings. I tell you, gentlemen, it is a worse calamity than the grasshoppers; they are said to come but once in ten years, but this wheat ring is permanent.

The election was close, but Washburn won by three thousand votes, about 8 percent. Donnelly claimed that widespread fraud had been used against him. There was evidence that he had been beaten by bribery and by the outright intimidation of voters who worked in the Minneapolis mills. However, Donnelly had neither the political influence nor the money to push his case, and the leadership of the Democratic Party refused to do so for him. In the end, Washburn took the seat in Congress and later became a U.S. senator.

After this defeat, the Anti-Monopoly Party in Minnesota fell apart. Elsewhere, too, the farmers' political activity subsided. The end of the 1870s brought better business conditions and a cycle of good crops in the Midwest. The popularity of the Grange declined, partly because of business failures by several Grange-organized co-ops, and for a while it seemed that the agrarian revolt was over.

4. POPULISM AT THE POLLS

IN THE DECADE OF THE 1880S, MINNESOTA BEGAN TO RE-
alize that it was an urban as well as a rural state. The popu-
lations of both St. Paul and Minneapolis more than tripled,
and by 1890 the two cities accounted for nearly a quarter of
the state's people. Sawmilling, powered by the Falls of St. Anthony, had laid the foundation for booming industrial growth.
With the expansion of railroads, wheat poured in from the
newly opened fields of the Red River Valley, Dakota Territory,
and Manitoba, and the flour milling industry at the falls soon
led the nation. Other kinds of processing also mushroomed,
along with manufacturing. There were meat-packing plants,
breweries, clothing factories, and machine shops.

Wealth pyramided into fortunes associated with names
like Washburn, Pillsbury, Weyerhaeuser, Cargill, and James J.
Hill. With a growing industrial labor force, a few unions also
appeared. The first ones were limited to small, highly skilled
crafts like tailors, printers, barrel-makers, and cigar-makers,
but by the early 1880s they were spreading to railroad engi-

neers and to the building trades. In the mid-1880s the expanding Twin Cities were shaken by the nationwide rise of a powerful union of all workers, known as the Knights of Labor. It advocated not only higher wages but broad changes in society, and, like the Grange, it admitted women workers, of whom there were many in the new clothing factories of Minneapolis and St. Paul. Like the Grange also, the Knights started as a brotherhood with echoes of Freemasonry and soon grew into a political force.

Minnesota farmers, embittered and discouraged by the stolen election of 1878, had also begun to regroup. A forthrightly political organization called the Farmers Alliance replaced the less political Grange as the leading voice for farm protest. In 1884, joined by rural Democrats, the Alliance endorsed Ignatius Donnelly in another closely contested but unsuccessful run for Congress. The Democratic Party as a whole, controlled by railroad magnate James J. Hill through St. Paul political boss Michael Doran, refused to support him.

By 1886 it was clear that a partnership between the Farmers Alliance and the Knights of Labor was a political marriage waiting to happen. At a convention held that year in Minneapolis, the members of the Alliance resolved "That the interests of all producers are identical; the millions who work on farms find their chief market and natural allies among the millions who toil in shop and factory. The degradation and impoverishment of either class is a direct blow at the prosperity of the other . . . That there are really but two parties in this State today—the people and their plunderers."

The city workers still wanted to deal with the Democrats, however, while the farmers favored starting a third party. A compromise was reached when the leaders of the two groups, Donnelly for the Alliance and John M. McGaughey for the

Knights, approached the two major parties with a series of agreed-upon demands. Those included a clean elections law, more effective regulation of railroads, an anti–child labor law, an anti-usury law, and state regulation of industrial safety (the first step toward workmen's compensation). Both Republicans and Democrats agreed to the program, and as election day approached, the platforms of the two parties were almost exactly the same. So was their performance after the legislature convened in 1887. Not one of the proposals was passed, leading Donnelly to declare in disgust, "This ought to be called Jim Hill's legislature."

Blocked politically, the newly organized workers turned to direct action. The years 1888 and 1889 saw two important strikes. The first was notable not for its size but because it was conducted by women. On April 18, 1888, 260 seamstresses employed by a Minneapolis manufacturer of work clothing walked off the job. The immediate cause was a cut in the piece-work rate at which they were being paid. It had already allowed only the fastest and most skilled workers to earn a living wage. In the background was a long list of inhumane working conditions and abusive treatment by their foreman. The leaders of the walkout were members of a "ladies protective assembly" of the Knights of Labor, but, though supportive, the Knights did not officially call the strike. As John McGaughey said, they thought the women "knew their own business best."

The strike was widely publicized in the Twin Cities by a young reporter named Eva McDonald, who was hired for the purpose by the *St. Paul Globe* and wrote under the name Eva Gay. Her description of conditions in the factory drew sympathy and indignation from many church people and women throughout the cities. They supported a boycott of the company's goods called for by the Knights of Labor, and eventually the company closed its doors. Most of the strikers had to find work elsewhere. McDonald went on to become an organizer and lecturer for the labor movement.

A year later the largest strike that Minnesota had yet seen began when Thomas Lowry, owner of the Twin Cities streetcar system, cut the wages of drivers from six to four cents per hour. Workers speculated that he needed to show eastern bankers a healthy profit margin in order to get capital for expansion. He was in the process of converting the old horse-drawn cars to electric power and building lines to the growing suburbs. The drivers' union called a strike immediately.

It was a disaster. Workers' organizations from the Farmers Alliance and the Knights of Labor to the smaller craft unions stood by the strikers, and there was widespread public sympathy, even among businessmen. But Lowry refused to negotiate. No one was going to tell him how to run his business, he announced. He enlisted help from the city police and brought in hundreds of "scab" drivers from Kansas City and other western towns. Wives of the strikers climbed on board many of the cars and talked earnestly with the new "cowboy" drivers about solidarity. Some of them quit, but the strike was broken. None of its leaders was rehired, and all other employees were forced to sign a nonunion, or "yellow dog," contract.

By then the influence of the Knights of Labor had already been lessened by the Haymarket affair in Chicago. That occurred in 1886, at a rally to support workers who were striking for an eight-hour workday. Police tried to break up the rally, a bomb was thrown, and although no evidence ever connected the Knights or anyone else with the bombing, public fear, mass arrests, and the hanging of four men who claimed to be anarchists was a sharp blow to the whole labor movement.

In Minnesota the declining Knights continued to push the eight-hour-day protests until 1890, when they, along with the trades and labor assemblies of both Minneapolis and St. Paul, held a meeting to discuss forming a Minnesota Federation of Labor. Among a wide range of organizations represented at that meeting was the Farmers Alliance. In the same year, farmers and workers again united in a third-party challenge that threw a sudden scare into those who controlled the two major parties. Under the name Alliance Labor Union Party, they elected a congressman and fifty-three state legislators. Their candidate for governor, Sidney M. Owen, polled an impressive 25 percent of the vote.

Elsewhere in the country, too, the Farmers Alliance had been growing in power. In the new wheat-raising regions of the Dakotas, Nebraska, and Kansas, and all across the impoverished states of the South, the movement was becoming a major political force. One of its best-known national spokesmen was Minnesota's longtime warhorse of farm protest Ignatius Donnelly. He had gained fame in 1890 as the author of a best-selling radical novel called *Caesar's Column,* and people who hardly knew where Minnesota was had heard of him and read his book.

The story was set almost a hundred years in the future—in 1988—and portrayed the collapse of American society in a bloody battle between the "haves" and the "have-nots." Instead of establishing freedom and equality in the country, the miserable masses of people fall under the control of a ruthless dictator who builds a concrete tower into which he dumps the bodies of the thousands killed in the struggle. *Caesar's Column* has led some late-twentieth-century historians to charge that Donnelly was anti-Semitic, since in the book he adopts the stereotyped view of Jews that was common in

Ignatius Donnelly, 1898

rural America at the time. Yet Donnelly also defended Jews against discrimination and once said, "A great nation, like all magnificent mosaic work, has room in it for all the race elements of the world. There is room here for Goth and Celt and Basque and African and Jew—yes, even for the Indians, if they can survive civilization."

The book was selling a thousand copies a week by 1891, when a national convention of farm, labor, and reform groups met in Cincinnati. Donnelly led those who favored a third party and succeeded in creating a national committee for a People's Party. Back in Minnesota, the new group quickly absorbed the Alliance Labor Union Party, and "Populist" became a household word.

In 1892 Donnelly confirmed his standing as the national voice of Populism when he wrote a ringing preamble to the platform adopted by the People's Party. In it he summed up the desperation and foreboding that had grown for a quarter century among western farmers and among miners, lumberjacks, and factory workers:

We meet in the midst of a nation brought to the verge of moral, political and material ruin. Corruption dominates the ballot box, the legislatures, the Congress, and touches even the ermine of the bench. The people are demoralized. Many of the states have been compelled to isolate the voters at the poling places in order to prevent universal intimidation or bribery. The newspapers are subsidized or muzzled; public opinion silenced; business prostrate, our homes covered with mortgages, labor impoverished, and the land concentrating in the hands of capitalists. The urban workers are denied the right of organization for self-protection; imported pauperized labor beats down their wages . . . The fruits of the toil of millions are boldly stolen to build up colossal fortunes, unprecedented in the history of mankind, and the possessors of these in turn despise the republic and endanger liberty. From the same prolific womb of governmental injustice we breed the two great classes—tramps and millionaires . . . A vast conspiracy against mankind has been organized and is taking possession of the world. If not met and overthrown at once it forbodes terrible social convulsions, the destruction of civilization, or the establishment of an absolute despotism.

The convention nominated James B. Weaver of Iowa for president, and in Minnesota Donnelly himself ran for governor. But neither in the state nor in the nation could the Populists alone get enough votes to dent the two-party system. The Minnesota Republican Party used the strategy that had succeeded in 1873 and brought a fresh face into the race for governor. In 1892 the newcomer was a Norwegian American congressman from Alexandria named Knute Nelson, known for successfully challenging the influence of the Northern Pacific Railroad. He was the first foreign-born governor that the state elected, although like every Minnesota governor since the Civil War, he was a veteran of the Union Army.

Nelson won by promising most of the same reforms that Donnelly did, and even as the nation sank further into the depths of a bitter depression in the mid-1890s, the hopes for a third-party victory remained dim. In 1894 Minnesota Populists again nominated Owen, and that year they reached their peak at the polls, leading the Democratic candidate but losing to Nelson. As the presidential election of 1896 drew near, the workers, the unemployed, and the poor were in almost open revolt against the conservative Democratic administration of President Grover Cleveland, while the Republican Party remained the voice of large corporations and the banking system and promised only more of the same.

A ray of hope appeared when western opponents of the gold standard gained strength in the Democratic Party. Called "bimetallism," the new proposal was to make silver as well as gold the legal backing for currency and bank credit, thus increasing the money supply by another route than printing greenbacks. Politically it had the advantage of strong support not only from the country's mass of debtors but from silver mining interests that were especially powerful in the new states of the West. "Silver" Democrats also had a promising candidate in a young congressman from Nebraska named William Jennings Bryan, who, like Donnelly, was a powerful orator. At the national Democratic convention in 1896, he swept to victory in the party while thundering at Republicans and bankers, "You shall not crucify mankind upon a Cross of gold!"

Along with coinage of silver, the Democrats adopted, at least in rhetoric, several other Populist planks. So the People's Party was faced with the choice of supporting Bryan or conducting a futile campaign of its own. Reluctantly, most Populist leaders agreed to "fusion" with the Democrats by nominating Bryan. They recognized that it probably meant the end of their hard-won third-party organization, and they were right. Fusion signaled the demise of Populism as a political force. It also appeared that the sacrifice had been useless, since even with Populist support Bryan was in the end defeated by Republican William McKinley.

In Minnesota the aging Donnelly fought against fusion and remained a Populist until his death four years later, on the first day of the twentieth century. The Democratic Party was still controlled by Hill in 1896, but the railroad baron opposed bimetallism. When the *St. Paul Globe,* the state's main Democratic daily paper, backed Bryan, Hill bought it and switched

its support to McKinley. No one was surprised when the Republicans carried Minnesota.

Although the national Democratic Party swallowed Populism at a gulp, it was never quite the same again. The first
step had been taken toward aligning the Democrats with the
interests of workers, small farmers, immigrants, and minorities. The Republican Party emerged from the election as the
unquestioned voice of the business community.

5. STRIKES AND STRIKEBREAKERS

THE GILDED AGE OF THE LATE 1890S WAS A TIME OF PROS-
perity, rising prices, and triumphant big business. In 1895 a
decision by the U.S. Supreme Court in an antitrust case gave
a green light to trusts and interlocking corporate combinations. The first months of the twentieth century saw the greatest one of all formed—on the Mesabi Range, where a sleeping
giant had been awakened. The vast wealth of iron ore there belonged to John D. Rockefeller, who had strong-armed it away
from hard-pressed Minnesota investors during the depression of the mid-1890s. In 1901 the banker J. P. Morgan, with
help from Rockefeller, Andrew Carnegie, and others, pulled
together the entire steel industry into a mammoth grab bag
of iron and coal mines, railroads, ore docks, Great Lakes shipping, and steel mills. The United States Steel Corporation was
the largest company in the country.

The growing power of such mighty combinations troubled
even conservative businessmen and citizens. From ordinary
workers it brought desperate and angry opposition. They

fought it with new forms of organization and new solidarity. All across the nation, and especially in the West, the stage was set for bitter showdowns. One of the first had already started in Minnesota.

Jim Hill had become known as the state's "Empire Builder" after 1893, when his Great Northern Railroad reached Puget Sound. In that year a young labor activist in Chicago named Eugene V. Debs organized the American Railway Union. Unlike the railway brotherhoods, under which engineers, firemen, brakemen, and conductors all belonged to separate unions, the ARU was the first attempt to organize an entire industry in a single union. Any employee could join—even those who trudged along with pick and shovel to maintain the tracks. Within a year there were 140,000 members. Many of them worked for the Great Northern.

During that time Hill had repeatedly cut wages. By the spring of 1894 the cumulative pay cuts were more than a third of what had originally been paid. There had also been repeated protests, pointing out that men were working twelve to thirteen hours seven days a week and that a single man, let alone a family, could scarcely live on the new rates. Yet when the ARU called a strike in April 1894, the strength of the new union and the determination with which the men acted caught the Empire Builder off guard. From St. Paul to Seattle, his trains stopped. At stations all across the Great Plains and the Rockies, passengers and freight were stranded, since at that time railroads were the only form of long-distance transportation.

At first Hill refused to meet with the strikers or their spokesmen, but it was clear that public sympathy was with the workers. There was no violence, and the union itself appointed committees to patrol the yards and prevent any damage to Hill's property. A union flyer advertising a rally in Minneapolis ap-

pealed to his sense of fairness: "Mr. J. J. Hill . . . has a reputation for honor and liberality that is now imperiled," it said. "By
one word from him all will be saved and peace restored." Governor Knute Nelson added his voice. In a letter to both Hill and
Debs he urged a settlement. At the end of two weeks, a group
of Twin Cities businessmen, led by Minneapolis mill owner
Charles Pillsbury, invited the two men to present their cases.
Hill could hardly refuse the request of his peers, and he further
agreed to their offer to arbitrate the strike. He may also have
underestimated the skill and persuasiveness of Eugene Debs.
The settlement restored some of the cuts in wages and hours,
but the real victory was in forcing Hill to listen to the union.

A few weeks later in Chicago the situation was very different. There, ARU members voted to support the striking
workers of the Pullman Palace Car Company and refused to
handle trains with Pullman-built cars. The railroads therefore
attached Pullman cars to mail cars and demanded that the
federal government break the boycott. President Cleveland
sent in the army; the U.S. Supreme Court declared the union
to be violating the antitrust laws; and the ARU was effectively
smashed when its leaders were jailed on charges of conspiracy
to restrain trade. Debs spent his six months in prison reading
the works of Karl Marx and when he was released began to
organize the Socialist Party of America.

The Twin Cities saw no more major labor struggles until 1901.
In that year the machinists of Minneapolis joined a national effort by the International Association of Machinists to achieve
a nine-hour day. Part of the package was an understanding
that employers would deal with workers through the union
and not discriminate against its members—an arrangement
that was beginning to be known as the "closed shop." The re-

sult was an iron-fisted response from the newly organized National Metal Trades Association, and the strike was defeated in Minnesota as elsewhere in the country.

Leadership for united action by employers against unions had come from machine shop owners in Minneapolis, and it quickly spread not only to the machine tool trade around the country but to the rest of the Minneapolis business community. The solid front against labor was sealed in 1903 with the organization of the Citizens Alliance, a league of the city's financial and industrial leaders to keep Minneapolis an "open shop," or nonunion, city. Employers who did not unite with the alliance were quickly brought into line by the city's banks, which threatened them with loss of credit. The power of this new semisecret organization was confirmed within a year when a strike for union recognition and an eight-hour day in the Minneapolis flour mills was defeated by hiring nonunion workers and housing them within the tightly clustered milling district at the Falls of St. Anthony. Guarded by police, the milling compound became a virtual fortress to which union pickets could gain no entry.

The Citizens Alliance and its ideology dominated Minneapolis for the next thirty years. That ideology was based on defining the right of individuals to market their labor whenever and wherever they choose as "part of the personal liberty of a citizen that can never be surrendered." As an "inalienable right," this freedom must be enforced by government with its police power. Others have asked why bargaining for wages is a right that cannot be surrendered by an individual worker, when stockholders freely surrender to a corporate "person" their own right to bargain as individuals. Thus an imbalance of power is created, even without the added force of a union of employers.

Tugger pulling slusher filled with iron ore from end of drift, about 1905

If there were stark differences in power between mill owners and their employees in Minneapolis, such differences were
even more overwhelming on Minnesota's iron ranges. Along
the Mesabi, armies of immigrant laborers were already turning
the green hills into a moonscape of yawning canyons flanked
by mountains of mine waste. Those workers were a polyglot
crew. The first to come, and the most skilled, were from Corn-
wall, Sweden, and Finland by way of older mines in Michigan.
The unskilled men who worked in the open pits were mainly
newcomers from eastern Europe. The largest number were
Finns, but there were also Italians, Croatians, Slovenes, and a
scattering from other Slavic states of what was then known to
bewildered census takers as "Austria."

There were towns along the Mesabi and Vermilion ranges,
but most of the workers lived near the mines in moveable clus-

ters of company-owned buildings that were known as "loca-
tions." Those who were lucky found beds in boardinghouses
that catered to men of their own nationality, where they could
talk and smoke together in off-hours. Pay was not for hours
worked but by "contract," a variation of piece rates through
which a foreman could favor some men over others by assign-
ing them to richer veins of ore. Mining is always dangerous,
and in the early years U.S. Steel took few pains to improve
safety. Between 1905 and 1910 an average of five out of every
thousand Minnesota miners died in accidents each year. That
did not count those who survived with lost arms and legs or
other crippling injuries.

The diversity of cultures and languages was a barrier to
unions, but the Western Federation of Miners (WFM), which
had already won pitched battles in Colorado and other states,
sent organizers to the range in 1905. By 1907 there were four-
teen locals. The leaders were the Finns, many of whom had
brought socialist leanings from their homeland. In July that
year a strike by workers on the ore docks in Duluth slowed
down shipments and led to a wave of layoffs in the mines.
Those were clearly targeted at union members and were
probably intended to force a strike. If so, the ploy was successful. By the end of the month more than ten thousand miners had refused to work without better pay and an end to the
hated contract system.

Oliver Mining Division of U.S. Steel hired private mine
guards who were immediately deputized by the sheriffs of St.
Louis and Itasca counties. The mine owners also asked the
governor to send troops to bar the strikers from picketing.
Governor John A. Johnson, a moderate Democrat, decided instead to go and take a look himself. What he saw of working
conditions in the mines appalled him, and after talking with

the strikers, he called for a meeting with the mine owners. He took no other action to help the workers, but his attitude defused a tense standoff and reassured local townspeople and businessmen, who were fearful of violence and hostile to the union. No troops appeared, and neither did violence.

Meanwhile, the WFM was hastily sending its best speakers and organizers to support the unexpected strike. Among them was the beloved Mother Jones, who toured the range towns and spoke at a mass meeting held in Duluth. As Debs had done in the Great Northern strike, the Federation of Miners urged its members to keep the peace and avoid damage to property. Nevertheless, after the dock strike was beaten and the mines needed more men, the owners brought in whole trainloads of new laborers, most of them immigrants straight from southeastern Europe. Returning strikers were turned away, and the Finns especially were permanently blacklisted. Angry and embittered, some took seasonal jobs in what remained of the lumber industry, and many started small farms in the stump-filled cutover of northern Minnesota and Wisconsin. From there they built a network of Finnish socialist organizations.

There was an uneasy peace in the mines for another nine years. The new immigrants quickly learned about forming unions, but the Minnesota Federation of Labor, which was suspicious of industrial unionism, refused to organize them. The WFM had faded from the scene, with many of its members joining the Industrial Workers of the World (IWW), commonly known as "Wobblies." They were like the earlier Knights of Labor in their aim of forming "one big union" and creating a new society, but they were more militant in their tactics. In 1913 the IWW supported a strike by dockworkers in Duluth, Superior, and Two Harbors and opened a recruiting office in Duluth. Two years later, however, there was still no organization among mine workers on the range.

War in Europe, which started in 1914, had increased the market for iron and steel, and the mines were operating at full capacity. Wages, however, had not gone up, and the contract system still fostered kickbacks and corruption among mine foremen. One day early in June 1916, a miner threw down his tools in disgust and shouted to others to join him. Soon hundreds of men were marching from town to town along the seventy-five-mile length of the Mesabi. The strike was on, carried by a wave of anger but without prior organization or planning.

As word spread, the IWW jumped into action. A team of organizers arrived to create Local 490 and open headquarters in the town of Virginia. From there they arranged strike activities, published manifestos, and distributed food to those who needed it. Meetings were held mainly at the Finnish socialist halls in various range communities. Once again Oliver Mining hired a small army of private guards, and once again they were deputized by a compliant sheriff. The mining companies refused to talk with IWW representatives. Their position was voiced by the *Duluth Tribune* of July 7, which denied that the work stoppage was truly a strike. "What is faced on the ranges and in Duluth," it declared, "is revolution, just that and nothing less."

In other ways the situation was different from that of 1907. The war had slowed immigration to a trickle, and there was no pool of unemployed labor to replace the strikers. Therefore breaking the union depended on fear, repression, and hunger. Also unlike 1907 was the attitude of townsfolk and other citizens on the range. They, too, had come to have grievances against the mining companies, and local businesses extended credit to the strikers until their suppliers in Duluth cracked down. In places like Hibbing demonstrations were allowed, and town police held off the furious mine guards.

There was violence that led to three deaths and many injuries but no mass killings. Representatives of the Minnesota Department of Labor later blamed nearly all the violence on police and mine guards, concluding that "if the private mine guards had been compelled to remain on the company property we do not believe that there would ever have been any bloodshed on the range." Women played an important part, from Wobbly leader Elizabeth Gurley Flynn, one of the most popular speakers, to Mikela Masonovich, who was injured and jailed along with her nine-month-old baby after "deputies" broke into the Masonovich home without a warrant. IWW organizers were arrested on flimsy charges to take them out of action, but more kept coming, and the strike lasted all summer. By August the end was in sight, but there was still a note of triumph in some verses written by an anonymous Wobbly:

The Miners of the Iron Range
Knew there was something wrong
They banded all together, yes,
In One Big Union strong.
The Steel Trust got the shivers,
And the mine guards had some fits,
The Miners didn't give a damn,
But closed down all the pits.
It's a long way to monthly pay day,
It's a long way to go
It's a long way to monthly pay day,
For the Miners need the dough,
Goodbye Steel Trust profits,
The Morgans they feel blue.
It's a long way to monthly pay day

For the Miners want two.
They worked like hell on contract, yes,
And got paid by the day.
Whenever they got fired, yes,
The bosses held their pay.
But now they want a guarantee
Of just three bones a day,
And when they quit their lousy jobs
They must receive their pay.
It is this way in Minnesota
Is it this way you go?
It is this way in Minnesota,
Where justice has no show.
Wake up all Wage Workers,
In One Big Union strong.
If we all act unified together,
We can right all things that's wrong.

The workers were running out of resources, however, and men with families were beginning to return to the pits. In mid-September the mine strike officially ended, but not the activity of the IWW. Perhaps touched off by the miners' defiance, smoldering anger at working conditions in the logging camps and sawmills across northeastern Minnesota burst into flame. In December a strike shut down the huge Virginia and Rainy Lake sawmill, and by early January it had spread to most of the state's lumber industry. In response, sheriffs in the northern counties created armies of deputies and virtually declared war on the IWW. Members and sympathizers were rounded up without cause and warned to leave the area. Those who headed for the Twin Cities found themselves blacklisted. Their identity was known as a result of lists supplied to the Citizens Alliance by paid informants who had infiltrated the IWW.

During the years that followed, through World War I and the 1920s, U.S. Steel adopted the systematic use of such informants, generally known as "labor spies." Combined with blacklisting, it was an effective weapon against union organizing. Yet it seemed that something else had been learned in the boardrooms, for there was a carrot also. Soon after the strike, pay was increased and the worst abuses were corrected. As more time passed, safety and working conditions improved along with better technology. Although for years the steel trust avoided paying taxes on the fortunes in iron ore that it was taking out of Minnesota, indignant citizens of Hibbing and other range communities forced it to pay property taxes on the exceedingly valuable land it owned. Therefore, the immigrant workers on the range could boast that their children, growing up American, had some of the best schools and public services in the state.

6. THE PROGRESSIVE ERA: FROM REVOLT TO REFORM

STRIKING WORKERS WERE NOT THE ONLY ONES ALARMED and angered at the growing power of megacorporations like U.S. Steel. Although turned back in 1896, the high tide of Populist protest left its mark on both major parties. A new movement for reform took its place among farmers, townsfolk, and small businessmen of the Midwest. In time this became known as "Progressivism." One sign of it in Minnesota was the election of a Democrat as governor in 1898—the first in forty years. His name was John Lind, and he was elected on a three-party fusion ticket, with endorsement by Populists and Silver Republicans.

While Minnesotans were still worrying over the creation of U.S. Steel, they received another shock. In November 1901, newspapers announced the formation of the Northern Securities Company. It was a four-hundred-million dollar combination that controlled all the major rail lines in the northwest quarter of the nation. The organizer behind this monopoly was Minnesota's empire builder, James J. Hill.

Jim Hill's massive red stone mansion on a river bluff above St. Paul overlooked the state capitol, and critics like Ignatius Donnelly had accused him for years of quietly controlling both of the state's major parties. Businessmen, however, generally regarded Hill as a benefactor. His railroad was well run and conservatively financed, and he was farsighted in encouraging industry and agriculture along its line. Moreover, after he had become an international financial power, he continued to make his home in St. Paul. Although many Minnesotans would have agreed that Hill was a "robber baron," he was at least their own homegrown robber baron.

Nevertheless, in 1901 there were still no automobiles, highways, or airlines to give competition to railroads, and the long years of struggle against monopoly rates and other abuses had left their mark on state laws and public feeling. A Minnesota statute forbade consolidation of competing lines within the state. So Republican Governor Samuel Van Sant, who had replaced Lind, told the attorney general to file suit against the Northern Securities Company.

Van Sant, a tubby ex–steamboat captain from Winona with a walrus mustache, seemed an unlikely protest leader, but he held his ground firmly. He called a conference of governors from South Dakota, Montana, Idaho, and Washington who met in Helena, Montana, and unanimously endorsed Minnesota's effort to break up the railway combination. This legal action failed in the courts, but it played well politically. The editor of the *Rock County Herald* in Luverne spoke for a majority of Minnesotans on November 29, 1901, when he wrote, "Quick to see and prompt to act, [Governor Van Sant] has declared in terms which have shaken Wall Street to its center, that no corporation in all the world has capital enough to trample under foot the expressed will of the people of the state of Minnesota . . .

Former president Theodore Roosevelt, running on the Progressive Party's Bull
Moose ticket, addresses a crowd at the Minnesota State Fair, 1912.

For many years it has been a question whether the people or
the Great Northern railroad were in control of the state. That
is the question now at issue . . . It will be a fight to the finish."

In February 1902, President Theodore Roosevelt rocked
the country by starting federal prosecution of the Northern
Securities Company as a trust in restraint of trade. Like Van
Sant, he also gained the enduring loyalty of Minnesotans. Not
only did the state support him by a vote of four to one for
reelection in 1904, but in 1912, when he split with Republican
president William Howard Taft and ran on the third-party Bull
Moose ticket, he carried Minnesota with a strong plurality in
no fewer than sixty-two of its counties.

This result testified also to a growing disillusionment with political parties and blind loyalty to them. A generation earlier the politician who switched parties was ridiculed as a man who could not make up his mind or was for sale to the highest bidder. (Such accusations had led Ignatius Donnelly to retort that the animal best known for not changing its mind was the jackass.) But in the early 1900s, as parties came to be widely regarded as the tools of special interest groups, the badge "independent" began to stand for high principles, and a vote "for the man not the party" was seen as a vote for clean government.

The campaign against the influence of parties pushed in several directions: giving voters instead of party conventions the power to choose candidates (the direct primary); giving voters themselves the authority to recall elected officials or to pass or veto laws (the initiative and referendum); streamlining the structure of local government (city managers and municipal commissions); and making many elections (judges and local offices) nonpartisan. Minnesota experimented with all of these except recall and the initiative and referendum. Its most radical step was a nonpartisan legislature, which was adopted in 1913 and reversed in 1973, after sixty years.

As early as 1895 Minnesota's senator Cushman K. Davis, who was revered throughout the country as an intellectual voice for conservatism, had demonstrated the widespread acceptance for change when he said,

> If I were asked to define the controlling political and social elements and questions of this age, I should unhesitatingly say that they are the present and ever-increasing necessity of regulating the internal concerns of the state by government . . . [There is] the debauchery of the electoral franchise; the discontents engendered by vast disparities in wealth and ac-

tual power; the impotence of the law to deal with some of the
most threatening elements of society and of the body politic;
[and] . . . the insufficiency of the state and federal constitutions, ordained, as they were, in other times.

In fact the years that followed, from 1900 to 1920, saw
the virtual reinvention of American government. Among the
things that became part of the fabric of American society at
that time were the direct election of senators, an income tax,
strong child labor laws, minimum wage laws, workmen's compensation, pure food laws, regulation or municipal ownership
of public utilities, conservation laws, and improved public
health programs. There was a complete overhaul of the banking and currency system with the establishment of Federal Reserve banks. Finally, there was woman suffrage and nationwide
prohibition of liquor.

In Minnesota the high tide of the Progressive era came in
1912. In just thirteen days that summer a special session of the
legislature ratified federal amendments relating to an income
tax and the direct election of senators. According to the *Minneapolis Journal,* those and other reforms passed at that time
"completely revolutionized the state's present political system."

On one progressive step, Minnesota dragged its feet. Although
in 1920 it joined the rest of the states in ratifying the Nineteenth Amendment, Minnesota had stonewalled the rights of
women for seventy years.

Woman suffrage had become a public issue at Seneca Falls,
New York, in 1848, just a year before Minnesota became a territory. In the decade of the 1850s, it was closely associated
with the abolition movement. However, in 1857 when the fran-
chise for blacks and Indians was being hotly debated at the

state's constitutional convention, the question of woman suffrage received no mention.

The loudest voice for women's rights in Minnesota at that
time was Jane Grey Swisshelm, a newspaper editor who made
her home in St. Cloud for six years. Already nationally known
when she came to Minnesota, Swisshelm is best remembered
for her intense attacks on slavery. She also championed wom-
en's rights, but suffrage was not at the top of her priorities. It
would come in time, she felt, but legal discrimination against
women embedded in property and family law was more urgent.

In 1869 when the Fourteenth Amendment gave the vote
to black men but not women, leaders of the national suffrage
movement split. The more gradualist group founded the
American Woman Suffrage Association, and the militants rallied around the National Woman Suffrage Association. In the
same year Minnesota saw the beginnings of a network of local
"friends of equality" groups, but scattered population and dif-
ficulty of travel kept them from uniting in a state organization
until 1881. Meanwhile, in 1875 Minnesota's men amended the
constitution by a narrow margin to allow women to vote in
school elections. In part this got through by clever wording
on the ballot to disguise the purpose of the amendment and to
make it an automatic "yes" unless "no" were written in. Voters
firmly slammed the door, however, on letting women vote in
municipal elections or on liquor control.

The Minnesota Woman Suffrage Association affiliated with
the more moderate AWSA, and in 1885 it got a boost when
the association's national convention was held in Minneapolis.
Getting the convention to Minnesota was engineered by a newcomer to the state, Dr. Martha G. Ripley, who had both political
savvy and national connections. She also negotiated an alliance
with the temperance movement in Minnesota, but that proved

to be a two-edged sword. The state's large immigrant groups, especially the Germans and Irish, were already dubious about woman suffrage, and its association with a possible prohibition law solidified their opposition. For women the liquor question was fundamentally an issue of reducing domestic violence.

In the early 1900s, with the reform wave rising and the country looking toward more direct democracy and less government corruption, the suffrage movement gathered strength. Its two branches had merged into the National American Woman Suffrage Association (NAWSA), and a new generation of leadership had stepped forward. Cannily, younger leaders, like Minnesota's Clara H. Ueland, emphasized the connection between women and morality: "Mothers, from the beginning, have been the dynamic force that makes for better homes and thus for a higher civilization . . . This intensive concern for home should be expressed in government . . . The greatest enemies of humanity and especially of women, are intemperance, prostitution and war. The suffragists believe that by their votes they can help in defeating those enemies."

Meanwhile, Minnesota's Scandinavian immigrants were becoming more receptive to woman suffrage as their own homelands started giving women an equal voice in government—Finland in 1906, Norway in 1913, Denmark in 1915, and Sweden in 1918. Other states also had given women the vote, including Wyoming, Colorado, Oregon, and Arizona.

But in spite of speeches, parades, petitions, and bills introduced session after session, Minnesota's legislators were unmoved. As one Progressive journalist wrote in 1910, "The special interest influence in Minnesota lawmaking has been unusually powerful and prolific of predatory results because it represented a combination of great corporations, each electing its quota of members and all uniting their forces in a single machine. These corporations included the steel trust, a number of railway systems known legislatively as 'the railroad ring,' all the liquor interests of the state, and a score of public utility companies from the larger municipalities."

A tireless supporter of woman suffrage was state senator Ole O. Sageng, a Norwegian American farmer from Douglas County. Opposition centered in the St. Paul delegation, controlled by brewer Theodore H. Hamm.

With the approach of World War I, there was another split in the suffrage movement. Younger women united in the Congressional Union, later called the National Woman's Party, determined to act at the national rather than the state level. Taking a cue from the fiercely militant British "suffragettes," they engaged in disturbing protests and civil disobedience. Chaining themselves to the White House fence, burning the president in effigy, and staging hunger strikes after being arrested, they stole headlines from horrified homemakers like Ueland. Nevertheless, the sometimes-brutal treatment given them in jails drew public sympathy. Minnesota's leading activist was Sarah Tarleton Colvin, a trained nurse, public supporter of birth control (then illegal in Minnesota), and active member of the Woman's Party.

When opposition finally crumbled with adoption of the Eighteenth Amendment (prohibition) in 1919 and the Nineteenth (woman suffrage) in 1920, all suffragists united in celebrating the right that had been delayed for seventy-two years. After that, NAWSA morphed into the League of Women Voters, while Colvin and her group went on to work for an equal rights amendment. Nevertheless, another fifty years passed before Minnesota's women had more than a token presence in government, lawmaking, or the courts. In 1923 four women took seats in the legislature and another was added briefly in 1929, but not until 1973 was that number reached again, and from 1945 to 1950 there were none.

7. WAR MAKES NEW ALLIES

FOR MOST FARMERS IN MINNESOTA, THE TWO DECADES BE-
fore World War I were a time of relative well-being. The landscape of bleak prairie homesteads had been transformed with
solid farmhouses and barns, silos, occasional windmills, and
growing woodlots. It was also the heyday of the small town,
whose main-street storekeepers and local banks depended on
the prosperity of farmers around them. In a world without automobiles or highways, those towns were the focus of rural
economic activity, especially if they had service from the network of rail lines that then blanketed the state.

The wheat belt had moved west to the Red River Valley and
the Dakota plains. There, single-crop farming—with its risks
and its dependence on cash crops and distant commodity
markets—was the norm, and there, farmers remained angry.
They had some reasons. The grading and pricing of grain was
still tightly controlled, as it had been since the 1870s, by a
powerful combination of railroads, millers, and grain mer-
chants. The center of the "ring" was the Minneapolis Cham-
ber of Commerce, later called the Grain Exchange.

A new challenge to this arrangement appeared in 1902 with the forming of the American Society of Equity. Instead of political protest it took the road of economic pressure, to be exerted through producers' cooperatives and commodity holding movements. Of most interest to Northwest wheat growers was the Equity Cooperative Exchange, which aimed at becoming a terminal grain-marketing organization fed by a chain of local cooperative elevators. It was a forerunner of the Farmers Union Grain Terminal Association (GTA), but the struggle was an uphill one. By 1915, realizing that it was outmatched by the Minneapolis monopoly, Equity was advocating state-owned terminal elevators to restore competition. With campaigns organized largely by Socialist Party activists, North Dakota voters twice amended their state constitution to allow for this, but the legislature refused to take action.

Recognizing that the name "Socialist" was not popular with farmers and that small parties faced enormous barriers, the supporters of the Equity proposal decided to use direct primaries and to take over the dominant Republican Party. Under the inoffensive name "Nonpartisan League" (NPL), they started to organize. At that point a charismatic leader appeared.

Arthur C. Townley had risked and lost everything on a mammoth crop of flax in a year when speculators forced the price down on the commodity market. Feeling bitter and cheated, he became the chief organizer for the NPL. He recruited a team of angry young farmers like himself and a small fleet of the inexpensive cars that Ford was beginning to turn out on the first assembly line. They made the black Model T and the NPL symbols of grassroots organizing as they bumped over wagon roads and into hundreds of farmyards from one end of the state to the other. It lit what has been called a "political prairie fire."

By the end of 1916, the League had about forty thousand members, and its endorsed candidates, who swept the primaries in June, had won most of the North Dakota state offices, including governor. It also had a solid majority in both houses of the legislature. Not everyone was happy. One prominent North Dakota businessman was quoted by the *St. Paul Dispatch* as saying, "The Nonpartisan League is a band of socialists, led by an anarchist, bent on the destruction of the country. It will set the state back twenty years, plunge it into an overwhelming debt, and make it the laughing stock of the nation. If it stays in power past the next election most of the businessmen will leave the state and let the damned anarchists run it to suit themselves."

Most Minnesota farmers had little sympathy for the NPL, but wheat growers in the northwestern part of the state shared the anger of those in North Dakota. The summer of 1916 saw organizers in their Fords heading eastward across the Red River and into Minnesota, where membership and support blossomed.

There was also much interest among socialist-leaning workers in the state's cities, mines, and logging camps. The socialist tide was rising in Minnesota following the election of 1912. While the country had chosen Democrat Woodrow Wilson for president, and Minnesota voted overwhelmingly for Theodore Roosevelt, Socialist candidate Eugene Debs received 8 percent of the state's vote and carried Beltrami County. Even this unusual record for a small party did not fully reflect its strength in places like Minneapolis and Duluth. That year Thomas Van Lear, a popular leader of the machinists' union and the Socialist Party, missed being elected mayor of Minneapolis only because the Citizens Alliance persuaded the Democratic can-

A Nonpartisan League meeting in Carver County, 1918

didate to withdraw and throw votes to the Republican. In 1914 four Socialist city councilmen did win election, aided by the new nonpartisan status of city offices, and two years later Van Lear became the mayor.

In Duluth the Socialist Party had three large locals. At the oldest one, founded by followers of Debs in 1902, English was spoken, but there were also Jewish and Scandinavian ethnic locals. By early 1918 the total membership was estimated at nearly a thousand. In addition, the Finnish Socialist Federation with its lecture halls, its two Finnish-language newspapers, and a Work People's College on the edge of Duluth was a major influence throughout northeastern Minnesota and northern Wisconsin.

Van Lear's election brought sharpened tensions in Minneapolis. Alarmed that they had lost control of city hall, the members of the Citizens Alliance mounted a fierce propaganda campaign, accusing the new mayor of disloyalty because he opposed U.S. entry into the European war. Unions, meanwhile, became more aggressive as they saw companies like Minneapolis Steel and Machinery making enormous war profits from overseas arms sales but offering no wage increases. Workers were also confident that Van Lear would not use the city police to break strikes as his predecessors had done.

The same restraint did not apply to the sheriff of Hennepin County nor to the Citizens Alliance, which organized its own volunteer army "to back up our boys at the front" immediately after war was declared in April 1917. This army, called the Citizens Auxiliary, consisted mostly of middle-aged warriors who spent the early summer training and conducting sham battles on the state fairgrounds. In September, when a major strike threatened, they were deputized by the sheriff and heavily armed.

The strike grew out of nearly thirty years of hostility toward the union-busting policies of the Twin City Rapid Transit Company (TCRT), which was still controlled by the Lowry family. For the most part streetcars continued to run with nonunion drivers, but the conflict lasted for the duration of the war, going through several phases and ending in a confrontation between the national War Labor Board and Minnesota authorities directed by Republican governor J. A. A. Burnquist. There was little or no violence in Minneapolis, but riots broke out at various times in St. Paul. Overshadowing the entire dispute was the loyalty issue and the wholesale repression of civil liberties by the Burnquist administration.

In Minnesota the patriotic fever that accompanied U.S. entry into World War I reached hotter levels than in almost any other part of the country. This was largely due to anxiety about the state's great number of German Americans and their opposition to fighting for England and France. They and immigrants from many other places had come to America to avoid being conscripted in the ceaseless wars of Europe, and they were not slow about saying so. In April 1916, one German American farmer from Wells, Minnesota, had written to Senator Knute Nelson in Washington: "It is a shame that we have people in Washington that go to church on Sunday and pray for peace and the next day they are in favor to sell more ammunition to kill people . . . I am an American citizen since 1871 and I am willing to help protect the American coast if some foreign nation tries to land troops on our coast but I am not willing to work fight and get killed for John Bull."

Less than a week after the U.S. declaration of war against Germany, a remarkable bill was enacted by the Minnesota legislature. It created a seven-member Public Safety Commission that was given power to perform "all acts and things necessary or proper so that the military, civil, and industrial resources of the state may be most efficiently applied toward maintenance of the defense of the state and nation, and toward the successful prosecution of war." As the state's premier historian, William W. Folwell, later said, "If a large hostile army had already been landed at Duluth and was about to march on the capital of the state, a more liberal dictatorship could hardly have been conceded to the commission."

Other people, too, clearly understood the powers implied in the law's vague and sweeping words. Judge John F. McGee of Minneapolis, an aggressive patriot, wrote to Senator Nelson: "When it goes into effect, if the Governor appoints men who have backbone, treason will not be talked on the streets of this city and the street corner orators, who denounce the gov-

ernment, advocate revolution, denounce the army and advise
against enlistments, will be looking through the barbed fences
of an internment camp out on the prairie somewhere."

The governor appointed McGee, and he quickly became
the leader and spokesman for the Public Safety Commission.
More moderate members, including former governor John
Lind, soon withdrew in protest. In seeking to aid the war effort, the Commission registered all aliens in the state; arbitrat-
ed labor disputes; investigated German-language textbooks;
closed saloons, dance halls, and poolrooms at certain times;
and forbade the serving of liquor to women. But the first real
test of its powers came on July 25, 1917.

On that day a crowd of between eight and ten thousand
people gathered in the heavily German town of New Ulm to
protest the law under which young men were being drafted
to fight in a foreign war. It was a thing that had never before
been done in the United States, and they questioned its con-
stitutionality. The elected officials of the city were present,
and the tone of the gathering was law abiding and earnest.
Mayor Louis A. Fritsche assured the crowd that "There can
be no objection to the holding of a peaceful meeting of this
kind." And city attorney Albert Pfaender urged compliance
with the law until it could be changed. He concluded, "Let
your actions be such that in the future those who would doubt
your loyalty will be forced to admit that yours was the true
Americanism."

The leaders of the meeting found that their faith in the U.S.
Bill of Rights had been naive. Governor Burnquist immediately and illegally removed from office all of the town and county
officials who had been involved. In newspapers and speeches
throughout the state, abuse was heaped upon the "traitors" of
New Ulm, and one editor went so far as to regret that the Da-

kota Indians did not "do a better job" when they attacked the settlers of the town in 1862.

Even sharper cruelty faced one German American farm family whose son had died in the trenches. His funeral at a country church in southwestern Minnesota was conducted in German. When the local newspaper editor learned of it, he huffed, "To employ [the German language] at the funeral of one who had laid down his life in the service of his country against the German beast is an insult to every patriotic citizen."

German Americans were not the only group who felt the heavy hand of wartime repression and hysteria. All aliens were under suspicion. Noncitizens of any nationality were prohibited from employment in public schools, and "hyphenated citizenship" of any kind was a thing to be shunned. Nor was suspicion of disloyalty limited to recent immigrants. It quickly became a weapon for attacking anyone who expressed criticism of government policies or raised issues of social injustice.

The Nonpartisan League was one such group. Although it officially supported the war, it also demanded that sacrifices be shared. When the U.S. government put a cap on the price of wheat to farmers but none on flour manufactured by the mills, the League urged that the government take steps to pass on the savings to consumers and to curb the "extortionate profits" of millers. The Minnesota Public Safety Commission started an investigation of the NPL, but what it did directly was little compared to its not-so-subtle encouragement of police repression and mob violence in local communities. Early in 1918 the NPL issued a press release in which it reported how an outspoken opponent of the war was "beaten to a pulp" by a crowd of loyalists. Instead of disavowing such action, the Commission's statement concluded, "The time is coming when even a disloyal utterance or lukewarm attitude will be resented by the American people in every section. There is no 'half way' citizenship that can live in these times."

The intimidation and vilification of NPL organizers and supporters reached its peak during the spring of 1918, when the NPL backed former Minnesota congressman Charles A. Lindbergh for governor in the Republican primary. Lindbergh had long contended that U.S. entry into the war was engineered by banker J. P. Morgan and other members of "the Money Trust" who had investments in Great Britain. Throughout his campaign the danger of mob violence prevented him from speaking in many communities, and nineteen counties forbade all League meetings and rallies. Lindbergh's life was repeatedly threatened.

Meanwhile, other League leaders were held in jail under indictments for sedition, all of which were later dismissed by the courts. There were numerous incidents in which organizers were beaten or run out of town, yet state authorities did nothing until a vigilante group in Duluth dragged a young Finnish draft resister into a waiting car. Later his tarred and feathered body was found hanging from a tree. The authorities ruled it suicide. This at last led Governor Burnquist to proclaim that mob violence would no longer be tolerated. Editor Gunnar Bjornson of the *Minneota Mascot* spoke for many conservative people when he commented drily in the issue of October 11, 1918, "By heck, we believe that the governor is right . . . We were beginning to think that the old constitution was but another of the historic scraps of paper that was valuable now only as a relic."

A month later the armistice was signed and the suspicions and accusations over the loyalty of thousands of law-abiding Minnesotans of German ancestry became only a memory. It was a long and bitter memory, however. Meanwhile, the rise to power of the Bolsheviks in Russia and the continued militance of unions and NPL farmers fanned further fear and stirred attacks upon "Reds" both in Minnesota and throughout the country.

In 1919 insurgent members from the Minnesota Federation of Labor, meeting in New Ulm, formed the Working People's Nonpartisan Political League. It included Socialists like Thomas Van Lear, who had been narrowly defeated for reelection as Minneapolis mayor, and labor activist William T. Mahoney of St. Paul. The next spring, meeting separately but working together, the two NPLs continued the strategy of capturing the Republican ticket in the elections of 1920. Although their candidate for governor, a handsome young dentist from Glencoe named Henrik Shipstead, who was a favorite with the farmers, came close to nomination, the entire slate was defeated in a campaign centered around charges of socialism and atheism. With growing tension between its two arms, the protest coalition continued to battle through the general election, running its leading candidates as independents. The result was a Republican victory, but the loose alliance of farmers and workers far outran the Democratic Party, whose candidates averaged only 10 percent of the vote. The anger of normally Democratic voters at the warmongering of the Wilson administration had made a fundamental change in Minnesota's political landscape.

8. THE RISE OF THE FARMER-LABOR PARTY

AS THE COUNTRY CAME OUT OF WORLD WAR I, PROTEST movements faced a time of agonizing decision. The Socialist Party of America, which had been the only meaningful third party since the collapse of the Populists, had maintained a firm antiwar position even though many of its members, along with its leader, Eugene Debs, were serving prison sentences under the Sedition Act of 1918. More fatal to the party were events in Russia from which came a powerful new ideological current. This forced American socialists to choose between democratic socialism and revolutionary communism. Radical labor unions faced a similar crossroads.

For Minnesotans the choice was most divisive in the northern part of the state. There, the strong Swedish and Finnish socialist groups opted for communism. Most IWW members also took the road of revolution. More conservative unions, mainly in the Minnesota Federation of Labor, had long rejected any political action, yet many of their members were boiling with anger at the continued violation of civil liberties and were drawn to the new Working People's Nonpartisan League. Among farmers there was also a spur to greater activism. In 1920 wartime crop prices crashed, plunging agriculture into a depression that lasted until World War II. At the same time the farmers' NPL was faltering under constant attacks and divided leadership.

Looking at their narrow defeat in the 1920 election, the two leagues took the obvious next step: they moved to create a party. Each hung onto its own organization, but in the election of 1922, their jointly endorsed candidates ran under the name Farmer-Labor Party. The time had come. Farmer-Labor candidate Henrik Shipstead won a U.S. Senate seat over the prestigious incumbent, Frank B. Kellogg, and two NPL congressmen were elected in western Minnesota. This was followed by another statewide victory the next year, when Farmer-Labor candidate Magnus Johnson won a special election called after the death of Republican senator Knute Nelson. So Farmer-Laborites faced the election of 1924 with two U.S. senators and two congressmen in office but a party that was no more than a divided constituency and a name.

It was a presidential year. An organization called the Farmer-Labor Federation was hastily put together, and a convention was scheduled to be held in St. Paul, with Senator Robert M. La Follette of Wisconsin, who was running for president on a progressive third-party ticket, as the keynote speaker. At that point, however, the new movement faced another and more dire question: what to do about the strong contingent of communist supporters who were known in northern Minnesota as the Working People's Party?

Already it was becoming clear that American communists were following the lead of their Russian colleagues in both policy and tactics. Their aim was a complete revolution in society, and nothing less. They were tightly organized, took orders from the top, and were loyal above all to their own movement. Loosely formed, grassroots-oriented groups that were willing to go a step at a time and work within the electoral system faced great risks in cooperating with communists. There was always the chance of being controlled by a unified, militant minority that had its own agenda and the even greater possibility of being falsely connected in the public eye with violence and subversion.

In Minnesota, however, there was another element to be considered. A large number of the state's communists belonged to the Finnish Socialist Federation, which, after some delay, had allied itself with the Communist Party USA, accounting for fully 40 percent of that party's membership. Controlling their own newspapers and already involved in local elections, the Finns were a substantial and well-organized block of voters and were notably independent of the party line directed from Moscow.

Leaders of the new Farmer-Labor Federation, faced with balancing these risks for the first time, took the gamble of admitting the Working People's Party to the convention. The result was disastrous. La Follette refused to attend, and in the election of that year Farmer-Labor candidates were identified by the press as tools of the communists. One of those candidates was the popular, young prosecuting attorney of Hennepin County named Floyd B. Olson, who was narrowly defeated in his run for governor. Another was the new Farmer-Labor senator Magnus Johnson, who also lost his race. There was even some question about whether Henrik Shipstead, the other senator, would remain allied with the party as it struggled to recover.

* * *

The last years of the 1920s were a time of business optimism and Republican dominance in Minnesota as in the whole country. While the Farmer-Labor Party licked its wounds from the defeat of 1924, several things gave it hope. Clearly it had nudged out the Democrats as the second party in the state. In this it was helped by the persistent depression in farm country. Crop prices remained low, and while cities prospered and modernized with cars, highways, skyscrapers, and radios, most rural Minnesotans lived without electricity and watched small towns grow smaller as cities grew larger. So even farmers who were normally conservative voted for Farmer-Labor candidates who pushed not for socialism but for government support of agricultural prices and for laws that would benefit the growing number of farm cooperatives.

The party leaders also developed a new and effective form of organization not seen in Minnesota politics before. Faced with state laws that strictly limited the power and functions of a political party, they scrapped the Federation, kept the party as a formal shell, and created a tightly run entity called the Farmer-Labor Association. Both individuals and groups could join it by paying a membership fee. It published a newspaper and other materials, and it conducted community programs, lectures, and classes throughout the state. Opponents accused it of being a sort of party-within-a-party that included the core intellectual leadership on its executive committee and controlled party policies. Today it might be called a think tank.

The same years saw changes on the far left. The communist opposition to the Farmer-Labor movement had become divided. Vladimir Lenin's death early in 1925 had triggered a contest to succeed him, not only as ruler of the new Soviet Union but as leader of world communism. By 1928, therefore, U.S. and Minnesota communists were split between followers of Josef Stalin and those of Leon Trotsky. In Minnesota the dominant Stalinist group, identified as the Communist Party (CP), faced powerful competition from Trotskyists, organized as the Communist League of America (CLA) and after 1938 as the Socialist Workers Party.

In October 1929, the scene began to change throughout the country. Within a year the economy collapsed, banks failed, businesses closed, and unemployment skyrocketed. The election of 1930 promised a new climate for protest politics, and there were other hopeful signs of a Farmer-Labor victory.

Party leaders had asked Floyd Olson to run again in 1928, but he had declined. In 1930 he felt ready. The years since his defeat in 1924 had added to his stature as an enemy of corruption and crime in high places—of which Minneapolis had plenty in the 1920s. In addition to his reputation as a prosecutor, he had built a wide network of personal friends and supporters that went far beyond the Farmer-Labor Party. They included people like lifelong Republican Jean Wittich, vice president of the state League of Women Voters, who stood ready to lead an All Party Volunteer Committee to elect Olson in the name of good government. He had also cultivated an image of moderation, dismissing issues of radical ideology like public ownership and corporate privilege.

Throughout his campaign he took the same path, talking vaguely of the need for change but avoiding specific examples. When the votes were counted he had received nearly 60 percent, his Republican opponent about 36 percent, and the Democrat less than 4 percent. It was more a victory for Olson personally than for the Farmer-Labor Party, and in spite of the lopsided vote, Farmer-Laborites still did not control the state. Conservatives, generally identified with the Republican

Party, held a majority in both houses of Minnesota's nonpartisan legislature, and Republicans were entrenched in most other statewide offices, such as attorney general, auditor, and secretary of state.

The term for state offices at that time was two years, and the legislature met biennially. Therefore, Olson had only one session between elections to make changes. In 1931 he achieved a modest public works program to create jobs and a strengthened Department of Conservation. Minnesota then had no civil service system, and a different party in control at the capitol usually meant a large turnover in state employees. Olson had broadened his appeal to voters by promising not to fire competent and experienced state workers, and he kept his word. However, jobless members of his own party, hard hit by the depression, were bitterly disappointed, and in time, as they overrode Olson's resistance, the patronage issue became a thorn in the side of the Farmer-Labor Party.

Probably the most important act of Olson's first term was a veto. The census of 1930 had reduced the state's congressional districts from ten to nine. In redrawing the districts Republicans had gerrymandered them to give almost certain victory to their own party. Olson's veto meant that in the election of 1932 all of Minnesota's congressmen ran at large, and five out of the nine sent to Washington were Farmer-Laborites. The election was exceptional in other ways also. With the depression steadily deepening, it saw Franklin Roosevelt elected president and running far ahead of all other candidates in Minnesota. Olson was next, with half the votes cast for governor in spite of Republican, Democratic, and Communist rivals. Vital to the work ahead was a majority of liberals in the Minnesota House, although the Senate remained conservative.

* * *

As the 1933 legislature opened, the nation's banking system staggered toward collapse and Minnesota was overwhelmed with a wave of farm foreclosures. In the western counties, where deepening drought added to the farmers' desperation, foreclosure sales were being stalled by mobs, and firebrands were urging farmers to march on St. Paul and physically unseat the legislators.

Between mid-1931 and mid-1932, farm income, already low, had dropped by half. Prices for crops often did not cover the cost of harvesting them. Yet while farm produce rotted in the fields, unemployed workers and their families went hungry in the cities. Direct action appeared to many law-abiding farmers as the only possibility. They asked themselves why, if laborers could strike and if bankers could declare their own "holidays" when threatened with disaster, farmers could not do the same.

The idea spread like wildfire and took shape in an organization called the Farmers' Holiday Association. It was formed in May 1932, with support and inspiration from the Farmers Union but no direct connection. The movement centered in Minnesota and Iowa, but branches also mushroomed in the Dakotas, Nebraska, Wisconsin, and Illinois. Milo Reno of Iowa was elected its president, and John Bosch, a farmer from Kandiyohi County, directed its activities in Minnesota. The purpose was to withhold farm products from sale until prices were equal to the farmers' costs, either through market forces or legal action. Other demands included a moratorium on foreclosures and lowering of interest rates on farm loans. Radicals like Bosch also called for abolition of the Federal Reserve System and a 100 percent tax on any profits made from a war, but most farmers were not ready for such fundamental change.

As with the earlier Nonpartisan League, membership was greatest in the western part of the state. Wealthier farmers in

Grant County farmers among the marchers to the state capitol, 1935
(George E. Luxton)

the south and the large farm cooperatives, especially those in
dairying, opposed the movement. Even coordinating the tim-
ing of withholding actions proved difficult.

Early in August 1932, a spontaneous strike that was started by dairy farmers around Sioux City, Iowa, resulted in the
blockading of highways, picketing, and violence. There were
similar incidents near Omaha and Des Moines, and in Minnesota highways were blocked around Worthington. An effort to
prevent farm produce from entering the Twin Cities petered
out quickly, but in November more than a thousand farmers
shut down the Swift Company packing plant in Marshall.

* * *

Elsewhere a few deaths and many injuries occurred, but in Minnesota no one was hurt during the farm strikes of 1932 and later in 1933. Bosch was an admirer of India's Mohandas Gandhi, and he recognized that violence only weakened the farmers' cause. His restraint was reinforced by the cooperative attitude of the governor. Bosch recalled that "Here in Minnesota we were doing a pretty good job . . . at least 50 percent of the paid-up membership of the national Farm Holiday Association came from Minnesota . . . Floyd Olson did everything and anything he could, as did [Governor] Bill Langer of North Dakota. None of the rest of the governors had the guts . . . But it didn't take long to see that we were getting nowhere with the strike."

Action by farmers was more successful in stopping foreclosure sales, whether simply by threats of violence or by the charade of "penny sales," where the community would unite to buy the property at auction for a token amount and return it to the owner. Bosch told of one foreclosure incident in Montevideo:

> A U.S. marshal was there, and I bet I had about 1,000 farmers . . . I told him that I could convince him that he should not proceed with the sale. "Well," he said, "it doesn't make any difference how much I agree with you, I must proceed" . . . Out in the hall where you couldn't identify [anyone], somebody would holler, "Let the son of a bitch out here and we'll cut a hole in the ice and push him down twice and pull him up once" . . . This type of thing, and he was white as a sheet. Well, it's a fact—we never hurt anybody. Finally, he called the U.S. district attorney, and I asked him if I could talk, and I said . . . "If you call it off, fine, but if you want us to manhandle him, if we have to, we have to. But there's going to be no sale." So they called it off. Not long after that I got a call from Floyd Olson . . . and he said, "John, you can't buck the federal government." Well, I said, "Floyd, we

did." And he said "You're going to spend the rest of your life in the pen." And I said, "Now, Floyd, up to now we've hurt no one . . . but if you want a civil war, if that's what you're aiming for, that's the way to get it."

Facing the very real threat of violence, Olson did not turn to police action but toward removing the immediate cause of anger. Although his legal authority was doubtful, he proclaimed a halt to all mortgage foreclosures for two months, while challenging the legislature to work on a moratorium law. Even rock-hard conservative senators had little choice. The mortgage moratorium they enacted would expire in two years, but other changes made during that session were more lasting. These included adopting a state income tax, reducing taxes on homesteads, barring the use of "yellow dog" contracts and court injunctions to fight unions, and sweeping conservation measures that took exhausted land out of production and created thirteen new state forests. Farmer-Labor initiatives for unemployment insurance and public ownership of power plants failed.

Through the summer and fall of 1933 the continuing crisis in agriculture riveted the country's attention, and another region-wide farm strike brought violence in neighboring states as farmers battled state troopers to keep highways closed to agricultural shipments. Olson's talent for mediation helped to calm tempers in Minnesota, and his leadership among other midwestern governors brought him national attention and the friendship of Franklin Roosevelt.

Confronted by industrial conflict, Olson showed the same restraint. The first major strike was in Austin, a corn-belt town near the Iowa border. There in the summer of 1933, some former Wobblies who worked in the hog-kill section of the Hormel meatpacking plant held a number of open-air meetings at which they organized the Independent Union of All Workers (IUAW).

Throughout the fall Hormel denied a wage increase, and in early November its workers voted to strike. Returning to the plant, they occupied it and refused to leave, staging the first of what became known around the country as "sit-down strikes." At first they threatened to shut off the refrigeration system, but, in a gesture of conciliation, they agreed to keep it running, thus avoiding major property damage. After a brief scuffle, the sheriff of Mower County called for help from the National Guard. Instead of sending troops, Governor Olson drove to Austin to mediate the strike himself. He succeeded. The workers won their pay increase, and soon the IUAW spread to other packing plants and industries in Minnesota, Iowa, and South Dakota.

Despite his success in preventing violence, Olson was attacked by the country's conservative press for his failure to protect property rights. Taking to the radio, he fired back, "Apparently the mistake made by me . . . was that I did not turn the machine guns of the state on some 2,700 citizens and create some widows and orphans." Most Minnesotans cheered.

9. WAR IN MINNEAPOLIS

FLOYD OLSON HAD ALWAYS BEEN A MAN WITH DEEP SYM-
pathy for the underdog, and as world and national events
moved toward a climax in 1934, he moved also. Hunger was
widespread; in the Twin Cities nearly one in three workers
was unemployed; and the country seemed held together only
by emergency relief measures. The Farmer-Labor convention
that met in March turned its back on moderation and adopted a platform of outright socialism. Olson was swept with it.
He declared,

> Now I am frank to say that I am not a liberal . . . I am what I
> want to be—I am a radical. I am a radical in the sense that I
> want a definite change in the system. I am not satisfied with
> tinkering. I am not satisfied with patching. I am not satisfied
> with hanging a laurel wreath upon burglars and thieves and
> pirates . . . I am not satisfied with that.
>
> I want, however, an orderly, a sane and a constructive
> change. I don't want any more visionary things any more than
> the hardest tory conservative wants it, but I know the transi-
> tion can take place and that of course it must be gradual.

His words were still ringing through the state when a new and deadly conflict broke out in Minneapolis. Minnesota industry had seen no major strikes since the early 1920s, and industrial unionism was nearly dead. Minneapolis, known nationwide for the effective wall put up by the Citizens Alliance against unions, was also known for some of the longest hours and lowest wages in the country. Now a powerful local of the Teamsters union, organized with Trotskyist leadership, was ready to challenge the thirty years of nonunion rule by the organized employers. As the year 1934 opened, the Teamsters were busy spreading membership in Local 574 to all nonunion workers whose occupations were touched by the trucking industry.

This violated the craft model of the International Brotherhood of Teamsters, but despite its opposition, low-paid and unorganized workers in Minneapolis warehouses, coal yards, lumberyards, wholesale groceries, gas stations, and many other businesses flocked to the Teamsters. Thus Local 574 became not only an industrial union but actually a union of all workers in everything but name. Likewise, the battle that is known to history as the truckers' strike, which began in Minneapolis with a successful coal yard strike in February 1934 and lasted off and on through August, was in fact a broad, labor-based struggle for social change.

Early in the year Local 574 had opened headquarters in a garage that served as command center, meeting place, and dispensary. There, service was supplied for automobiles that picketers used to get around quickly and blockade truck movements throughout the city. There also a volunteer brigade of some three hundred women, called the "Ladies' Auxiliary" of Local 574, operated a soup kitchen that provided emergency rations and other help to those who were down and out and

Using tear gas during truckers' strike, Minneapolis, 1934

later gave first aid and temporary care to workers hurt in the street fighting. Led by activist women, some of whom were associated with the Trotskyist group, this female auxiliary served as a bridge between the workplace and the wider community, reaching into churches and cultural organizations and arousing broad support for the strikers.

As they had done in 1917, the leaders of the Citizens Alliance organized their own militia to oppose union pickets, but this time the odds were more equal. There was no state military support for the Alliance, although they did enlist help from Minneapolis police. The crowd of striking workers was joined by many of the angry unemployed. Within days the streets of Minneapolis became a bloody battleground.

Pressured by both Olson and the National Labor Relations Board, the employers agreed to negotiate but would make no concessions, and after a lull of a month, street confrontations resumed. This time weaponry escalated from clubs and fists to firearms and brought the death of two strikers along with the wounding of more than sixty others. As governor, Olson was forced to keep the peace and make sure that essential services and deliveries of food and medicine were maintained. He declared martial law and put the National Guard to patrolling the city. Both picketing and nonessential truck movements were prohibited. Even when the role of the state was limited, its power inevitably tipped the balance against the union. Meanwhile, Olson was furiously attacked by the press and by legal action of the Citizens Alliance, which appealed to the courts for an injunction to lift martial law. Relying on his skill and experience as a courtroom attorney, Olson argued and won the case himself.

At that point the governor was rescued by his unofficial alliance with Democrats in the New Deal administration. Where political, military, and legal power failed, economic pressure succeeded. The Minneapolis banks that supported the Citizens Alliance owed millions to the federal Reconstruction Finance Corporation, and that agency threatened to recall its loans unless the strike was ended. Within a few days the Teamsters found their union recognized and most of their demands met.

The election in the fall of 1934 returned the Minnesota House to a conservative majority and doomed the governor's program for the legislative session of 1935 to defeat. As a whole that program still leaned toward the creation of a welfare state rather than a transfer of power away from the major corporations. Its most radical feature was a proposed constitutional amendment authorizing the state to engage in businesses of various kinds.

Olson himself let it be known that he was interested in the 1936 race for U.S. senator. In the closing days of 1935, however, a thunderbolt struck the Farmer-Labor Party. An emergency operation at Mayo Clinic revealed that the governor had advanced pancreatic cancer and would live only a few months.

Floyd Bjørnstjerne Olson died in August 1936, at the age of forty-four. Historians have agreed that he ranks first among the state's governors, given the critical times he faced and his way of bringing warring factions together both in and outside his own party. He helped to create and steer the most important and long-lasting third-party movement to exist in a state where such movements are no novelty.

The only son of a Swedish mother and a Norwegian father, Olson shared the heritage of political leaders like Knute Nelson, John Lind, Magnus Johnson, Henrik Shipstead, and Charles Lindbergh, who had made Minnesota known as a new Scandinavia. Behind his rugged appearance, his electric presence, and his intense activity were years of ill health. Many of his days had been shadowed by pain—pain that he soothed with generous amounts of alcohol. Raised in a rough, working-class neighborhood of Minneapolis, he could be both crude and charming. His magnetism for people, including a number of political opponents, rested on a keen understanding and a sympathetic firsthand knowledge of human frailties.

Olson's last year in office had seen yet another history-making strike. At the Strutwear Hosiery Company in Minneapolis, a craft union limited to highly skilled knitters faced an attack by antiunion management and turned for support to more than six hundred unorganized production workers, mostly women, who had never been allowed to join the union. The result of an eight-month standoff was a broadening of union membership to all employees and ultimately a closed shop contract. The victory owed much to hundreds of pickets recruited by the Workers Alliance, an organization of the unemployed put together by Communist Party activists, and to university students who volunteered for picket duty. Despite the Citizens Alliance, Minneapolis was becoming a union town—but a town whose culture of community solidarity reached far beyond the workplace. Old-time labor leaders could hardly recognize it, and some found it threatening.

The successful Minnesota strikes helped set the pattern for a nationwide wave of union organizing and labor battles during the late 1930s. Most of it followed industrial lines, matching labor with the growth in size of industries and new technology. The result was passage of the National Labor Relations Act (1935), which limited the power of employers in fighting unions, and formation of the Congress of Industrial Organizations (CIO), which competed fiercely with the largely craft-based and more conservative American Federation of Labor (AFL).

In Minnesota itself this revival of industrial unionism had a great impact on the Iron Range. The depression had cut deeply there. By 1932 the mines had been largely shut down, and 70 percent of the workers were either unemployed or working no more than six days a month. In Duluth related industries like the steel plant, the ore docks, and Great Lakes shipping were affected, and the unemployment rate of more than 30 percent was the highest of any city its size in the country.

The road to unionization of the mines remained a long one. After passage of the National Labor Relations (Wagner) Act in 1935, communists and other radical unionists did some local organizing for the Mine Workers Industrial Union, but little came of it. Meanwhile, in 1936 a Steel Workers' Organizing

Committee (SWOC) was formed within the Amalgamated Association of Iron and Steel Workers, and in 1937 it became a part of the national CIO. The battle to organize the steel mills was long and hard fought, but with war looming in Europe and the demand for steel rising, U.S. Steel surrendered and was eventually followed by the independent companies known collectively as "little steel." The miners on the range were not included in this initial struggle, although one of the leaders in the bitter battle with "little steel" was a Finnish communist from the Iron Range named Arvo Gus Halberg, better known as Gus Hall. During the war years of the 1940s, SWOC undertook a widespread organizing campaign in Minnesota, and by 1946 collective bargaining had been established in the mines. By then the Amalgamated Steelworkers had become the United Steelworkers of America.

The Communist Party remained strong in northern Minnesota in spite of its internal divisions and the alienation of many Finns through an effort by the party in 1930 to politicize a network of Finnish cooperatives. Some communist Finns also listened to a plea from Soviet recruiters to move to Russian Karelia, taking tools and expertise to struggling timber industries there. Between 1931 and 1934 some ten thousand Finns migrated from the United States and Canada, including many from northern Minnesota and Wisconsin. A few returned in disillusionment, but most became tragic victims of the Stalinist purges in the late thirties.

By 1935 the rise of Nazism to power in Germany had prompted a sudden shift in world communism toward cooperation and forming of a "popular front" with other antifascist movements. In Minnesota the Farmer-Labor Party responded to this change by dropping the bar to communist membership in the Farmer-Labor Association, and as a result the party's 1936 convention had a sizable bloc of delegates who were communist sympathizers.

In that year an immigrant miner from the island of Corsica named John T. Bernard was elected to Congress from the eighth district in northeastern Minnesota. He had run on the Farmer-Labor Party ticket, but he had strong communist ties. On one of his first days in Congress, he had to make a choice that defined who he was.

Civil war had just started in Spain, and a democratically elected government was under attack by fascist rebels who were receiving military aid from Mussolini's Italy and Hitler's Germany. The United States refused aid to the Spanish government. Communists, however, saw the war in Spain as a prelude to wider conflict and were working hard to raise supplies and arms for the "loyalists." As Congress convened, the Democrats presented an embargo bill that would block any aid shipment from a U.S. port. They hoped to rush it through on a unanimous resolution in time to stop several ships that were poised to leave for Spain. Under great pressure and against all advice from Farmer-Labor friends, "Little Johnny" Bernard blocked their plan with the only "no" vote in the House. Being what he later called "a premature antifascist" made him a pariah in Congress and cost him the next election, but eventually the Corsican rebel became a radical folk hero on the Iron Range.

10. FELLOW TRAVELERS AND MERGER

THE ELECTION OF 1936 MARKED THE HIGH TIDE OF BOTH the Farmer-Labor Party and Roosevelt's New Deal. The president received 60 percent of the vote in Minnesota, and the Farmer-Labor candidate for governor, Elmer A. Benson, came in at 58 percent, riding a wave of emotion generated by Olson's death. Also elected was Ernest Lundeen, the Farmer-Labor candidate for U.S. Senate. Thus the party had a governor, two senators, and five of Minnesota's nine congressmen. Yet both the nation and the state stood at a turning point.

During the later half of the 1930s, U.S. attention became fixed on the growing threat of fascism in Europe, while in Minnesota bitter divisions over this and other issues tore the Farmer-Labor Party to shreds. As the 1938 election approached, public demand for change remained strong, but protest politics was fractured among at least four groups. Each of those groups was subject to sudden veering with the shifting winds of world events.

Minnesota Stalinists followed the line of the national and international communist parties (Comintern) in forming a "popular front" against Nazism. They supported and infiltrated the new industrial unions and called for intervention in the Spanish war. However, with the announcement in August 1939 of the short-lived Hitler-Stalin pact, they abruptly reversed themselves on foreign policy and took a neutralist stand. A further blow to the many Finnish communists in northern Minnesota was the Soviet attack on Finland in November 1939 and the so-called "winter war" that followed. Minnesota's powerful communist movement never really recovered.

Trotskyists remained strong in Minneapolis, boosted by their leadership of the successful truckers' strike. Like the Stalinists, a number of them joined the Farmer-Labor Association when it removed its bar to communist membership. After the election of 1938, however, they withdrew from the Farmer-Labor movement and formed their own Socialist Workers Party. It ran local and state candidates. The assassination of Leon Trotsky in Mexico during the summer of 1940 robbed them of ideological leadership, and the U.S. Alien and Sedition Act, passed in the same year, struck down their local leadership. Prosecuted under this so-called Smith Act, Minnesotans Vincent (Ray) Dunne, Carl Skoglund, and Grace Holmes Carlson went to federal prisons or were ordered deported.

The socialists, led nationally by Norman Thomas, had kept their influence in the Farmer-Labor Party through several aging but radical leaders—people like Susie Stageberg of Red Wing and Henry Teigan, a veteran editor of Nonpartisan League and Farmer-Labor publications. With the rise of fascism and the approach of World War II, socialists again, as in 1918, faced an identity crisis. The movement essentially split apart over its traditional antiwar position and the grim specter of Nazism.

In Minnesota many of the moderates who remembered the bitter legacy of persecution in World War I and who had voted for Floyd Olson remained unhappy with the drift toward war. They made the state notable for what was coming to be called "isolationism." Olson himself had declared during his last months, "In every war England makes new international law . . . I wouldn't trade the life of one youth for the whole damned 'freedom of the seas.'" Senator Henrik Shipstead was also immoveable in his opposition to intervention in Europe, as was the state's new senator, Ernest Lundeen. Minnesotans listened also to the words of Charles A. Lindbergh Jr., the aviator son of the Minnesota congressman who had so strongly opposed World War I and had helped found the Farmer-Labor Party. Young Lindbergh, who had gained world fame as the first man to fly solo across the Atlantic, spoke on behalf of the America First Committee, an antiwar group that had heavy conservative support accompanied by anti-Semitism.

To these conflicting forces was added the bitterness of personal feuding between Farmer-Labor Party leaders. As governor, Benson, an unyielding champion of reform, was bluntly radical and showed none of Olson's finesse. He was opposed by Hjalmar Petersen, who had been Olson's lieutenant governor and felt entitled to succeed him. Petersen had been ignored by a clique that controlled the Farmer-Labor Association and whom he believed to be communists and "fellow travelers." Therefore he challenged Benson in the 1938 primary. It became one of the ugliest campaigns within the state's memory, marked by both red-baiting and anti-Semitism. In the final election disgusted voters reversed

Governor Elmer Benson speaking at the Farmer-Labor State Convention, Duluth, 1938

the landslide of 1936 and elected a brilliant young Republican newcomer named Harold E. Stassen.

The victory of Stassen, who at thirty-one was the youngest man ever to become governor of a state, was the first step toward a new generation of moderates and antifascists in the Minnesota Republican Party. It also signaled a fundamental shift in U.S. politics. The gap between foreign relations and internal policy was narrowing, as was the gap between regional and national politics and economics. A third party limited to one state was becoming unworkable. Minnesota, swept by the mobilization for World War II, approached the 1940s as a state whose industries were still rooted in the Upper Midwest, serving agriculture and processing raw materials. It emerged from the war as a diversified manufacturing and high-tech state. Local companies like General Mills, 3M, Honeywell, Minneapolis Moline, and Northern Pump were becoming industrial conglomerates with interests and influence that reached far beyond the state and region.

Coming changes in the political climate could be seen by 1940, when Stassen's keynote address at the Republican National Convention helped secure the nomination of the internationalist upstart Wendell L. ("One World") Willkie as the presidential candidate. In the same year the Farmer-Labor Party lost both senators. Shipstead became a Republican to the delight of antiwar hardliners in that party; Lundeen was killed in a plane crash. To fill out his term, Stassen appointed Joseph H. Ball, a Twin Cities journalist who had been beating the drums for support of Britain, which stood alone against Hitler after the fall of France. Stassen himself was reelected in 1940 and again in 1942 with the understanding that he intended to resign and accept a commission in the navy. He did so—and went on to become the chief architect of the United Nations charter.

The tide of world affairs that divided Republicans also tugged at the Farmer-Labor Party. In June 1941, Germany invaded the Soviet Union. Again the Communist Party obediently reversed itself, and those sympathizers who were still entrenched within the Farmer-Labor Association became ardent interventionists and then all-out supporters of the war and the Democratic administration. Meanwhile, farmers who had been part of the Farmer-Labor coalition were enjoying boom times and had more interest in the maneuvers of the congressional Farm Bloc to maintain high prices than in changing an unjust system.

Former governor Elmer Benson remained Minnesota's leading Farmer-Laborite. He was widely accused of being a communist—or at least a "fellow traveler"—but opponents found it hard to make the image stick. In spite of his outspoken radicalism, Benson was a wealthy small-town banker from western Minnesota with a Norwegian heritage. Others in the party, like Abe Harris, Roger Rutchick, Marian LeSueur, and her daughter Meridel, were easier targets. Another was Viena Johnson, who, as secretary-treasurer of the Farmer-Labor Association, became the first woman to exercise statewide power in a major Minnesota party.

The attack on Pearl Harbor in December 1941 brought the United States into the war as an ally of both Britain and the Soviet Union. Through the next four years the pressures pushing the Farmer-Labor Party toward consolidation with Minnesota's puny Democratic Party became steadily stronger. They reached a high point with the approach of the presidential campaign of 1944, with leftists fearing for the defeat of Roosevelt and ordinary voters beginning to see communists as "good guys" in the light of Russia's heroic defense against Hitler. Although Roosevelt had carried Minnesota in the three previous presidential elections, the White House became increasingly concerned over his prospects in 1944 and, viewing Minnesota as a swing state, urged a merger of the two liberal parties there.

As with Minnesota Republicans, a new generation of younger voices was being heard in the Democratic Party also. One of them was a college teacher named Hubert Humphrey. Bursting with energy, a warm liking for people, and joy in addressing a crowd, Humphrey was later called "the Happy Warrior." He was defeated in the 1943 election for mayor of Minneapolis, but he made a good race. The next year, when Benson showed willingness to talk about a merger of the parties, Humphrey became a negotiator on the Democratic side, although tradition has greatly exaggerated his role. A cautious agreement was at last reached, one of the breakthroughs being the decision to keep the names of both parties. Thus the Democratic Farmer Labor Party (DFL) was born in April 1944.

The two wings of the new party were in agreement at the national Democratic convention a few months later. Both supported vice president Henry A. Wallace of Iowa as Roosevelt's running mate, but Wallace was replaced by Harry S. Truman. The choice was crucial, for although elected to a fourth term, Roosevelt died unexpectedly in April 1945, and Truman became president.

In 1945 World War II ended and the nuclear age began. No longer was the United States only one of the allied nations; it now held the awesome power to devastate or dominate the entire world. Shock waves of fear and distrust cracked the foundations of world cooperation. After the collapse of Germany, the Soviets took immediate steps to protect their devastated country by occupying Eastern Europe. This led British prime minister Winston Churchill to declare that an "iron curtain" had been drawn across the continent. In September 1946, Henry Wallace replied that the United States had no moral or legal right to dominate Europe or to deny the Soviet Union a buffer zone on its border.

By the end of 1946, the country was polarized between those who clung to the vision of democratic world government represented by the new United Nations and those who believed that encircling and defeating the Soviet Union was the necessary next step toward a "free world." In an open letter to the president, former Minnesota governor Elmer Benson stated,

> It is a most terrifying fact to the people of the country that today, after one short year of peace, there is more official talk of war, and more actual preparation for it, than at any time before the beginning of the Second World War . . . We are the mightiest power on earth; we need fear nothing except our own rashness. Yet by our senseless piling of atomic bombs we are paralyzing half the world with the sickening fear of another war.

The following March the president called for military intervention in Greece and Turkey, where communist insurgents were fighting the established governments. In what became called "the Truman Doctrine," he announced the U.S. right to interfere in the internal affairs of any country where communism threatened to become dominant. The Cold War had begun.

The year 1945 had also seen Hubert Humphrey elected mayor of Minneapolis, replacing a notably corrupt administration. The office was nominally nonpartisan, but Humphrey's whirlwind efforts to clean up the city made him the leading figure on the Democratic side of the DFL. He also became a champion for the emerging issue of human rights.

It was still a time in which half the country was legally segregated, including the nation's capital city and all its armed forces. Blacks were the main targets of prejudice but not the only ones. In 1946 popular author Carey McWilliams named Minneapolis "the capital of anti-Semitism in America." By unwritten rules, Jews were barred from most upscale restaurants and conservative social clubs, while the city's business and professional establishments largely excluded them. As mayor, Humphrey brushed aside these customs with decisive personal gestures, like entering one of the city's most exclusive restaurants with black journalist Carl Rowan at his side. His immediate effort to get a Minneapolis fair employment practices ordinance was defeated in the city council. He tried again and got it passed in 1947.

In Minnesota human rights was politically safe and an issue on which the two wings of the DFL could still agree, but international questions and control of the party overshadowed it. At the state convention in 1946, the tightly organized leftists took over the party offices to the dismay of Humphrey and his Democratic supporters. Reelected mayor in 1947, Humphrey took up the fight to gain control of the new party, declaring, "We're not going to let the political philosophy of the DFL be dictated from the Kremlin. You can be a liberal without being a Communist, and you can be a progressive without being a Communist sympathizer, and we're a liberal progressive party out here. We're not going to let this left-wing Communist ideology be the prevailing force because the people of this state won't accept it, and what's more, it's wrong."

Humphrey and his close corps of friends and supporters, including Orville Freeman, Arthur Naftalin, and Eugenie Anderson, set to work organizing, precinct by precinct. Using tactics borrowed directly from the leftists in the party, they swept the DFL all the way to the state convention in the spring of 1948.

The national Democratic convention came together in July of that year under a cloud of gloom. Truman was unpopular. All polls predicted victory for Republican candidate Thomas E. Dewey, and Democrats were split. Henry Wallace had announced his intention to run on a progressive third-party ticket, and the so-called "Dixiecrats" from the southern states were poised to withdraw over the question of human rights.

As a matter of hard reality, the nation's postwar bid for global leadership in a largely non-white world meant that the United States would have to give up its historic customs of racial and religious discrimination. In Humphrey's words, "We cannot use a double standard. Our demands for democratic practices in other lands will be no more effective than the guarantee of those practices in our own country." The question was whether the time had yet come when Democrats and the country's voters would accept a strong civil rights platform. Liberals thought they would, and Humphrey was chosen to lead the floor fight. In his most famous speech he told the convention, "To those who say that we are rushing this issue of civil rights—I say to them, we are 172 years late. To those who say this bill is an infringement on states rights, I say this—the time has arrived in America. The time has arrived for the Democratic Party to get out of the shadow of states rights and walk forthrightly into the bright sunshine of human rights."

When he finished, wild cheering broke out, and the platform was adopted. The vote was close, however, and delegations from four southern states left the convention to nominate Strom Thurmond of South Carolina for president. The four-way election of 1948 (Truman, Dewey, Wallace, Thurmond) ended with Truman's victory and proved to be one of the most dramatic upsets in American history.

Minnesota's Elmer Benson became the national campaign manager for Henry Wallace under the name Progressive Party, while in his own state the DFL backed Truman. Humphrey ran for the U.S. Senate against Joseph Ball, the Republican incumbent, who in 1947 had been a principal author of the antilabor Taft-Hartley Act. The Progressive Party nominated James Shields. Humphrey's identification with the civil rights issue and the support of labor elected him as Minnesota's first-ever Democratic senator. And there was no doubt that he was a Democrat. The "FL" in the party's name had become no more than a historic memory.

11. A NEW PROGRESSIVE ERA

IN THE TWENTY-FIVE YEARS BETWEEN 1950 AND 1975, MIN-
nesotans enjoyed a time that can be compared in some ways to
the quarter-century between 1895 and 1920. It saw prosperity,
growth, and bipartisan cooperation on reform measures. As in
the 1890s, third-party revolt had been effectively sidetracked,
but both major parties had been changed by it. For the DFL
this was the "Humphrey era" of reform and idealism; the state
wielded more influence in national politics than ever before.
Minnesota Republicans were influenced by the legacy of Harold Stassen, who served as one of President Dwight Eisen-
hower's closest advisors ("Secretary of Peace," some called
him) and by a series of liberal Republican governors—most
notably Luther W. Youngdahl (1947–51), Elmer L. Andersen
(1961–63), and Harold LeVander (1967–71).

Changes in Minnesota's governmental structure in the mid-
twentieth century also followed the pattern of the earlier Progressive era as part of a nationwide wave of reform. This was
prompted by U.S. Supreme Court decisions in 1962 and 1964

on apportionment of representation. As in many other states, Minnesota's city voters had been grossly underrepresented, and since 1913 the state legislature had been firmly controlled by conservatives from rural areas. The court decisions that led to a rule of "one person, one vote" launched a fierce battle over redrawing the state's legislative districts that resulted by 1972 in a new balance of power. For the first time the DFL had a majority in both houses.

Party designation was restored to the legislature in 1973, ending the sixty-year experiment in nonpartisanship. Flexible sessions were also adopted, allowing a de facto annual session instead of the single long session every two years that had been the custom, and a new "open meeting" law did away with closed committee hearings. A single ticket for governor and lieutenant governor was created. This prevented situations where the two officers, running separately, were of different parties. Even earlier, in 1963, the governor's term had been lengthened from two to four years.

In 1971 moderate progressivism reached a peak during the administration of Wendell L. Anderson in what was widely cheered as "the Minnesota miracle." The term referred to shifting a large part of the tax burden for public schools and other services from local governments to the state, thus equalizing education between poor and wealthy districts and achieving a more progressive tax structure. The "miracle" had bipartisan support, as did the creation in the late 1960s of a Metropolitan Council to meet the need for coordinated planning and administration in the seven-county metropolitan area, which would soon be home to half the state's population.

Economically, those decades saw crops multiplied many-fold by mechanized equipment, chemical fertilizers, insecticides, and herbicides. They saw taconite mills built to replace the exhausted mines on the Mesabi, and they saw the St. Lawrence Seaway, a century-long dream of bringing ocean shipping to Duluth, realized at last. The same years also saw the melting of differences between country and city lifestyles, as power lines spread to every corner of the state, freeways made travel faster, and rural schools were consolidated. By the end of the 1950s, nearly every household had a television set with its fantasy world of sex, celebrity, consumption, and limitless expectations.

There was a dark side to these years, however. Fear was an ever-present shadow. Nuclear bombs with unimaginable deadliness were tested, and the Cold War's delicate balance of terror threatened to tip with each new crisis as the United States reached to stamp out communism in places like Korea, Iran, Cuba, and Vietnam. For Minnesotans the steady militarization of the country was largely invisible, but even in rural places backyard bomb shelters were built and children crawled under their school desks in air raid drills.

Fear of another kind was also being whipped up. St. Paul author Patricia Hampl recalls that as a child in the 1950s she often lay awake in terror of "the *communists* who lurked in the dark." Since 1945 the witch hunt for radicals and their sympathizers had been gaining strength. Well-publicized "investigations" told the American people that Hollywood, university campuses, government offices, and especially the CIO unions were honeycombed with "commies" who were intent on betraying the United States into the hands of the Soviet Union. It was a replay of the Red Scare that had followed World War I, but it lasted longer and went deeper. One difference was the presence in the 1950s of the Federal Bureau of Investigation (FBI). Under the direction of J. Edgar Hoover it had become a national secret police. Thus the hunt for "Reds" was more organized and far reaching than ever before.

In February 1950, Senator Joseph R. McCarthy of Wisconsin told a Republican gathering, "I have here in my hand a list of 205 . . ." The names on it, he claimed, were all employees of the U.S. State Department who were known to be Communist Party members but were still employed in shaping American foreign policy. His claim was never verified, but McCarthy went on to become the witch-hunter-in-chief of the early 1950s, and his name became associated with the times and the hysteria. Not until he attacked the Pentagon in 1954 was he discredited and censured by Congress.

Minnesota was not immune, but patriotism and suspicion of dissent never reached the fever pitch of World War I. Many states required special loyalty oaths of all teachers and public employees, but when Minnesota's Republican governor C. Elmer Anderson (1951–55) let it be known that he would veto any such law, the question was dropped. Senator Humphrey, however, facing reelection in 1954, amended the national Communist Control Act to formally outlaw the Communist Party, which he declared, "isn't really a political party, it's an international conspiracy." Although unconstitutional and repressive, the action was excused by Humphrey's friends because, they said, it called McCarthy's bluff.

A number of Minnesota communists served time in federal prisons, either because they admitted party membership or because they refused to betray comrades. One of them was Gus Hall, who had become one of the party's national leaders. He served eight years after conviction under the Smith Act. Party records were destroyed in fear of subpoenas. Both nationally and locally, "Commies" or their sympathizers were weeded out of unions or, if that were impossible, competing unions were supported. Although disillusioned by the brutal authoritarian regime in the Soviet Union, younger Marxists were buoyed by the communist takeover in China and the writings of Mao Tse-Tung. Maoism began to take its place beside Leninism or Stalinism as a distinct ideology. Most radicals, however, turned away from economic and class-based issues to more pressing questions of peace and human rights. "Movements" were becoming more significant than parties; identity politics was safer and more acceptable than class war.

By the mid-1950s a new and vocal peace movement had begun to take shape. Its early protests were directed at the ongoing testing of nuclear weapons conducted in the earth's atmosphere by a number of nations, for such weapons were no longer a U.S. monopoly. As people learned that radioactive fallout from the tests affected everybody, the bands of protesters at test sites grew. Lacking any sort of electoral channel, they took to direct action and civil disobedience patterned on the campaigns of Gandhi in India. It never became a mass movement in Minnesota or elsewhere, but there was much public sympathy, and national peace organizations represented in the state included the Fellowship of Reconciliation (FOR) and the War Resisters League (WRL). In 1963 their pressure achieved a treaty that ended aboveground testing and was signed by most of the countries involved.

Meanwhile, the peace movement and its techniques of nonviolent resistance had become closely identified with the struggle to end racial segregation in the South, which was also blocked by local laws from wielding any electoral power. Beginning with the Montgomery bus boycott in 1955, support, ideas, and recruits supplied by the peace organizations had profoundly influenced Martin Luther King Jr., the young black minister who soon became the leader of the ongoing revolution. Minnesota was distant from Alabama, and although the Twin Cities' black population had increased by 41 percent during the war years, it remained small compared to other urban centers. Nevertheless, Minnesota was uniquely linked to the ongoing civil rights struggle through Humphrey, who had pushed it at an early stage in Minneapolis and carried it to the national Democratic Party in 1948.

Building on the direct protest actions of nearly a decade, Humphrey led the bitter fight in the U.S. Senate to achieve passage of the landmark Civil Rights Act of 1964. It was accompanied by the great "freedom summer" of confrontations in southern states and followed with the Voting Rights Act of 1965. But by 1966 the civil rights movement itself was being upstaged by demands for "black power" and racial autonomy. The summer of 1967 saw fierce rioting in cities across the country, along with increasingly violent repression of Black Panthers and similar groups. In Minneapolis there was disorder, but it was minor compared to rioting in places like Newark and Detroit.

Waves started by the struggles of black people lit resistance among other disadvantaged groups. In 1968 a group of young Indian militants living in the Twin Cities formed the American Indian Movement (AIM). They demanded tribal autonomy for Native Americans within their own communities and restitution for the conquest and genocide perpetrated by European Americans. American Indians had been Minnesota's largest racial minority until World War II, and the founders of AIM, including Russell Means, Dennis Banks, and the Bellecourt brothers, sprang from the state's main indigenous tribes, the Anishinabe (Ojibwe or Chippewa) and the Dakota (Sioux).

Actions followed in rapid succession, including the occupation of Alcatraz Island in San Francisco Bay (1969), the opening of cultural survival schools in the Twin Cities, and in 1972 a continent-wide march on Washington to mark the "Trail of Broken Treaties," ending with occupation of the Bureau of Indian Affairs (BIA) offices. In 1973 violence between Indian people and federal officers broke out at the community of Wounded Knee in South Dakota, and in 1974 a resulting eight-month trial of AIM leaders, held in St. Paul, ended in dismissal of charges against them.

Just as the call for abolition of slavery in the nineteenth century had awakened a demand for the rights of women and had marched hand in hand with the suffrage movement, so the civil rights campaign of the twentieth century was also followed by a new wave of feminism with demands for equality in pay, politics, and social attitudes. The 1964 Civil Rights Act outlawed discrimination on the basis of sex as well as race, and, prodded by women's organizations, Governor Karl F. Rolvaag created a Minnesota Commission on the Status of Women the next year. But not until 1970 was a Minnesota chapter of the National Organization for Women (NOW) formed. Its first mission was to dust off the Equal Rights Amendment, which had languished since the 1920s, and push for passage by a legislature that included just one woman among 201 members.

In 1971 women's caucuses in both major parties were formed and the nonpartisan Minnesota Women's Political Caucus was created, followed in 1972 by the election of six women to the House of Representatives. They included Joan Growe, who went on in 1974 to become secretary of state, an office she held with distinction for twenty-four years. Others elected in 1972 were legislators Linda Berglin and Phyllis Kahn. The following year Minnesota became an early adopter

A student protest against U.S. invasion of Cambodia at the University of Minnesota, May 1972 (*Minneapolis Star Tribune*)

of the Equal Rights Amendment, which ultimately failed to be approved by enough states for ratification.

The great issue that drew protest to the streets and also moved it back to the voting booth was the Vietnam War. Although half of Vietnam was controlled by native communists, the United States had tried for years to prop up an unpopular puppet government through material aid, military advisors, and CIA intrigue. By the early 1960s failure was clear. The choice was to abandon Vietnam or send American troops. The death of President John Kennedy slowed the decision, but after winning the election of 1964 in a landslide against pro-war Republican Barry Goldwater, Lyndon Johnson declared two wars—one on poverty and one in Vietnam.

Minnesotans felt closely involved through Hubert Humphrey, who had given up his Senate seat to become U.S. vice president in 1964. For the next four years he abandoned his longtime stand for peace wherever possible and became a champion of the Vietnam War. As casualties mounted and Americans watched the horrors of modern warfare on their TV screens for the first time, resistance rose, and people poured out for massive antiwar demonstrations. Martin Luther King Jr. moved to join them.

Meanwhile, another U.S. senator from Minnesota, Eugene J. McCarthy, was becoming a national spokesman for opposition to the war. Until then he had been an unremarkable DFL politician, but his passion for peace and his eloquent words stirred the country's young people. Late in 1967 McCarthy announced that he would be a candidate for president in 1968, saying,

> Instead of the language of promise and of hope, we have in politics today a new vocabulary in which the critical word is war: war on poverty, war on ignorance, war on crime, war on pollution. None of these problems can be solved by war but only by persistent, dedicated, and thoughtful attention.
>
> But we do have one war which is properly called a war—the war in Vietnam, which is central to all of the problems of America. A war of questionable legality and questionable constitutionality . . .
>
> What is necessary is a realization that the United States is a part of the movement of history itself; that it cannot stand apart, attempting to control the world by imposing covenants and treaties and by violent military intervention; that our role is not to police the planet but to use military strength with restraint and within limits, while at the same time we make available to the world the great power of our economy, of our knowledge, and of our good will.

President Johnson decided not to seek another term in 1968, and Humphrey announced his candidacy. Robert Kennedy also joined the race. In Minnesota the DFL was split wide open between the supporters of Humphrey and McCarthy. The assassination of King in early April 1968 brought demands and demonstrations in the Twin Cities but none of the rioting that broke out in other places, and the killing two months later of Kennedy left the Democratic presidential nomination a contest between a pair of Minnesotans. At the convention in Chicago, police attacks on antiwar demonstrators further inflamed the issue and cast a long shadow over the campaign of Humphrey, who received the nomination and continued, with little enthusiasm, to defend Johnson's record. Minnesotans were again reminded of the volatile condition of the country on Labor Day weekend, when a street battle broke out between young blacks and St. Paul police.

The split among Democrats resulted in a narrow victory for the pro-war Republican candidate, Richard M. Nixon, who had first won national attention as a red-baiter. McCarthy announced soon afterward that he would not run for another term as senator. His move left the way open for Humphrey to return to the Senate in 1970, where he remained until his death in 1978. Meanwhile, Gene McCarthy retired to the life of a writer and poet, although he was several times a symbolic candidate for president.

The war in Southeast Asia continued and expanded, and protest in Minnesota reached new intensity. The Honeywell Project, started in 1968, laid periodic siege to the state's largest military contractor and its manufacturing of cluster bombs. There was also increasing resistance to the draft. In July 1970 eight young men were arrested while attempting to destroy draft records in Winona, Little Falls, and Alexandria. The case of the "Minnesota 8" became a celebrated antiwar cause, but action at the polls seemed futile after the reelection of Nixon in 1972. Not until the explosion of the Watergate scandal and Nixon's resignation in 1974, followed by the fall of Saigon to communist forces early in 1975, did the long agony of war in Southeast Asia end.

12. DEEPENING DIVISIONS

DESPITE THE FEEBLENESS OF ORGANIZED ELECTORAL PRO-
test during the Cold War years, the country witnessed a not-
so-quiet revolution in values and lifestyle. American memory
usually links it with the 1960s. In reality it extended from the
late 1950s through the '70s, and its message that "the personal is political" still echoes in the polarization of politics.

For some it appeared as a generation gap, but the widespread alienation from American society and the determination
to create an "alternative" culture went far beyond the nation's
youth. It found expression in dress, drugs, sexual freedom, and
social rebellion, but it was also deeply political and economic.
Those aspects of it were embodied in a declaration by the Students for a Democratic Society at their convention in Port Huron, Michigan, in 1962. The Port Huron Statement marked the
birth of a "New Left," at least as radical as the old Marxist left
but less doctrinaire and less disciplined. In the Upper Midwest,
with fresh memories of farm revolt, another expression of the
new revolution was a back-to-the-land movement.

Jack Miller had left a promising career in journalism to return with his wife and son to the small community of Mill-
ville in southern Minnesota, where his grandparents had lived.
There he hoped to raise a family and publish a regional magazine that would speak for those who were seeking an alternative way of life in the country. In 1972 he wrote,

> We need to free ourselves from a whole way of living and look-
> ing at the world. The values, the assumptions, the systems that
> we have been given simply do not make us the kind of people
> we want to be, do not give us the kind of a world we want to
> live in.
>
> For many of us the first great disillusionment came with the
> Vietnam War. We saw our forces killing innocent people and
> destroying a beautiful and quiet land in order, we were told, "to
> give these people the right to choose their own form of govern-
> ment without outside coercion." Our killing apparently didn't
> count as "outside coercion" . . . For others it was seeing the
> way our nation gobbles up precious resources and despoils the
> land, all in the name of a grosser Gross National Product. For
> still others, it was seeing the emptiness and the sterility of the
> American Way of Life: a mindless, fleshless consumerism.

In the context of nuclear terror and a dawning awareness of
environmental destruction, the old ideologies seemed shop-
worn. The problems lay in the whole of industrial civilization,
rooted in a monetary economy. Words like "anarchism" and
"libertarianism" were tossed around in early issues of Miller's
North Country Anvil. There were also nostalgic references to
Minnesota traditions like "agrarianism" and "populism," but
as yet there seemed no single word that encompassed the
powerful yearning for a more simple-living, community-based,
and earth-friendly society. "It is hard to convey the optimism
and revolutionary zeal we possessed and felt we were building,"

says Minneapolis community leader Dean Zimmerman, who as a young man was deeply immersed in the various causes and conflicts of those years.

The movement toward community was embodied throughout the country in the growth of so-called "hippie communes." Minnesota had a number of them. The best-known one began in Minneapolis in 1968 but soon moved to Georgeville, a rural community in southern Stearns County. At its height there were about forty-five members, sharing possessions, income, and work. They lived by gardening and the sale of handicrafts. One young woman recalled,

> Like the rest of nature, Georgeville flowered and grew in the summer. Starting our own garden was an important step on the road to freedom; freedom from the prices and poisons of commercially grown produce, freedom from the necessity of working an 8:00–5:00 schedule to support ourselves . . . When winter came, the group narrowed to about 12 people. Winter was like being on the edge of a cold distant planet. We huddled around a wood stove, talking of gods and gardens, of governments that must fall to be replaced by peaceful cooperatives.

Georgeville and communities like it provided the seedbed for a whole new growth of consumer cooperatives. The crop was larger in Minnesota than elsewhere, probably because the state's century-long tradition of farm cooperatives gave it a well-cultivated field to take root in. This was true even though many young leaders of the "new wave" health food stores with their organic produce and bins of beans and whole grains were unaware of that history and certainly saw no relationship between giant co-op distributors like Land O'Lakes and their own efforts.

Many people were drawn by the freedom and equality of collective management and the independence of living outside "the system." For others it was the vision of gradually replacing the greed and conflict of capitalism with a cooperative commonwealth. Political paths were blocked; now economic efforts looked more promising. Four years after the first small co-op opened business on a back porch in Minneapolis, Minnesota had some thirty-five such enterprises. Most, but not all, were in the metropolitan area. Most featured "natural" foods, and they included a bakery, several restaurants, and a wholesale grocery warehouse that was central to supplying the network.

But just as Stalinists of an earlier generation had seen in northern Minnesota's Finnish co-ops a source of power and outreach, so dedicated New Leftists of the 1970s saw the new wave co-ops as a made-to-order tool. In May 1975 a tightly organized group of leftist sympathizers took over a warehouse in south Minneapolis. They announced their intention to operate the distribution system for the benefit of the "working classes," which apparently meant offering more staple supermarket groceries and meats in place of "elite" (mostly vegetarian) health foods. They gave the other co-op members at the warehouse a choice of joining them or leaving.

When word got around, co-op people from all over the Twin Cities arrived, and there was a confrontation that lasted through several days and many debates and shouting matches. At one point the police were called, but no one really wanted violence, and in the end the co-op network simply formed another wholesale operation, leaving the leftists to struggle on for a year or two as their warehouse slowly emptied. Nevertheless, the so-called "co-op war" proved a turning point for Minnesota's new wave stores. They continued to multiply, reaching more than seventy by the end of 1976, with a distribution system that served four states.

There was no unifying ideology, and people joined and patronized co-ops for many different reasons. With growth the new wave stores gradually lost their countercultural innocence and evolved into business-style organizations. To survive in the American world meant more than supplying people with healthy food at the lowest possible cost; it also meant competing with vast chains and reams of advertising.

The revolution seemed stalled. In 1962 the authors of the Port Huron Statement had written, "The message of our society is that there is no viable alternative to the present. Beneath the reassuring tones of the politicians, beneath the common opinion that America will 'muddle through,' beneath the stagnation of those who have closed their minds to the future, is the pervading feeling that there simply are no alternatives, that our times have witnessed the exhaustion not only of Utopias, but of any new departures as well."

The same year had seen the publication of *Silent Spring,* a book by biologist Rachel Carson that shook the United States and the world with chilling examples of the destruction of nature's living systems by the new pesticides. "Ecology" quickly became a familiar word. In 1970 another book, *The Limits to Growth,* showed that with expanding human use, the earth's resources were already running out. The message was neither complicated nor uncertain.

Minnesota, meanwhile, had a problem that showed just how slow and painful change would be. Since early in the 1950s wastes from the first large taconite plant at Silver Bay on the north shore of Lake Superior had been dumped into the lake. It was thought that these "tailings" would simply settle to the

Tailings delta, Silver Bay, 1963

bottom and stay there, but by 1968 it became clear that they had not. Cloudy patches of green water were seen for miles along the coast, and there were reports of fish dying. In 1970 the U.S. government brought suit. As the case made its slow way through the courts, it was learned that taconite has microscopic fibers much like those in asbestos and posed a potential danger to all the communities along the shore that drew their drinking water from Lake Superior. Those included the city of Duluth. In 1974 Judge Miles Lord ordered an immediate stop to the dumping. The Silver Bay plant shut down, but millions of dollars and some three thousand jobs were at stake. The order was reversed by an appeals court and six more years went by before the pollution was stopped.

By the mid-1970s the vision of peaceful nuclear power as a limitless source of energy "too cheap to meter" had also faded, replaced with fear of radioactive waste for which there was no safe means of disposal. In the long shadow of these milestones, various environmental movements had gathered urgency and merged with the dreams of an alternative lifestyle. Terms like "appropriate technology," "local self-reliance," "land steward-ship," and "small is beautiful" (the title of another influential book) became familiar. But more powerful than any words was a picture of the fragile blue globe of Earth seen from the blackness of outer space during the moon landings of 1969.

Slowing or reversing the destruction of the earth's bio-sphere demanded immediate and fundamental changes in per-sonal life as well as in the life of nations throughout the world. Controlling the explosive growth of human population was only one of them; controlling an economy that needed con-stant growth to keep functioning was another. These looming changes, combined with the freewheeling lifestyle called for by the alternative movement and with feminist demands for an end to subordination of women were profoundly troubling to social and religious conservatives everywhere. Minnesota became a classic battleground for the opposing views.

Minnesotans had always been churchgoers. Religion was closely intertwined with ethnic ties, and both had histori-cally been important in the state's political life. In the 1920s William B. Riley, pastor of the First Baptist Church of Min-neapolis and a leading fundamentalist, had established the Northwestern Bible Schools in opposition to the University of Minnesota's teaching of evolution. He told his congregation to "Unite in your demands that the University which belongs to us all shall not become the personal property of a dozen regents or a hundred Darwinized or Germanized deceived and faithless professors."

Billy Graham, the nation's best-known evangelist in 1970, had been a protégé of Riley, had served as president of the Northwestern Bible Schools from 1947 to 1952, and for years after that kept his headquarters in Minnesota. It was a portent that he had close ties with Republican president Richard Nixon and was often a guest at the White House.

The deepening division in the state along lines of religion and the nature of human rights was highlighted in 1973, when Justice Harry Blackmun, one of two Minnesotans on the U.S. Supreme Court, wrote the majority opinion in the case of *Roe v. Wade*, the decision that made abortion legal. The issue was already becoming the rallying point for a powerful political movement led by Minnesota Citizens Concerned for Life, which was founded in 1968 to oppose repeal of the state's antiabortion law. For more than three decades the MCCL would be a constant presence at the capitol and later in the councils of the Republican Party, while the question of abortion, in one form or another, was never absent from legislative sessions. Meanwhile, protest politics assumed a new face, as antiabortion and antiwar demonstrators, all against killing that they saw as immoral, marched under opposing banners.

Equally divisive was controversy over the rights and roles of lesbian women and gay men, which erupted shortly after the new feminism challenged the sanctity of the traditional, or "patriarchal," family structure as portrayed in the Bible and most of human history. Thus by the mid-1970s the struggle for human rights took in not only racial, ethnic, and religious groups but gender and sexual preference also. Increasingly, political lines were being determined by the interests of one or more opposing groups rather than by economic class or by the needs of the community as a whole. With identity and single-issue politics more dominant, the "big tents" of the two-party system became dysfunctional, yet a shift to smaller parties and proportional representation seemed nearly impossible.

13. A SWING TO THE RIGHT

AS POLARIZATION INCREASED, MINNESOTA'S SECOND PRO-gressive era was drawing to a close. As during the first such period, Democrats and Republicans had shared political power, and control of the governor's office had alternated between them. But at the midpoint of the 1970s, as Minnesota was celebrating its national reputation as "a state that works," it was also preparing to turn back to its historic Republican preference. Of thirty-three governors who had served since statehood, twenty-three had been Republican and only seven Democratic. The year 1972 was the first in which Democrats elected both a governor and majorities in both houses of the legislature. In the next thirty years, the governor's office would be occupied by three Republicans, one middle-of-the-road Democrat, and one fiscally conservative member of a third party.

In 1976 Minnesota senator Walter Mondale was chosen as the running mate of Jimmy Carter and became the second

Minnesotan to serve as vice president of the United States. DFL governor Wendell Anderson resigned, and his successor, lieutenant governor Rudy Perpich, appointed him to fill out Mondale's term in the U.S. Senate. The move was unpopular, and in 1978, in what is often known as "the Minnesota Massacre," Republicans swept the state, electing Al Quie as governor and sending two Republican senators to Washington. In 1980 the whole country followed Minnesota's sharp turn to the right in electing Ronald Reagan as president.

In addition to the Democratic slate, Reagan was opposed by two other candidates. John Anderson, a moderate Republican, rejected the party's growing conservatism and ran as an independent, and Barry Commoner, a leading environmental scientist, was nominated by the Citizens Party. Although neither received many votes, they testified that protest politics was still alive in the country. Meanwhile, feminists cheered the choice made by Walter Mondale, whom the Democrats nominated to oppose Reagan in 1984. For the first time in U.S. history, the candidate of a major party named a woman as his running mate. She was Geraldine Ferraro of New York.

In Minnesota the Republican Party had officially changed its name to "Independent Republican" following the Watergate scandal and Nixon's resignation. Soon, however, its more moderate members found themselves being outspent and out-organized by an alliance of Christian and pro-business rightists. Some of the more liberal Republicans turned their support to Rudy Perpich, who was governor from 1982 to 1990.

Minnesota's first Catholic governor, Perpich was the son and grandson of Croatian immigrants. He was also the first governor to come from the Iron Range. That region was no longer identified with flaming radicalism. Depleted resources and competition from global trade led miners there to see their interests as parallel to those of industry. Perpich had served as governor for two years after Wendell Anderson left for the U.S. Senate but was defeated in 1978. Four years later Perpich won the Democratic primary over the more liberal candidate endorsed by DFL party regulars.

Often lampooned by his detractors as "governor goofy" because of his unorthodox ideas, Rudy Perpich was hard to classify. Some saw him as a populist and others as a conservative. A staunch friend of women in government, he chose Marlene Johnson as his running mate, and she became the state's first female lieutenant governor, starting a pattern that has persisted ever since. He appointed Judge Rosalie Wahl as the first woman to serve on the state's supreme court, and he continued appointing female judges until for a brief time the court had a majority of women. Despite his Catholic heritage, he avoided divisive social questions like abortion and gay rights, but on economic and labor issues, particularly in his last term, he leaned toward business.

Worried environmentalists and other protesters who were represented by neither party in state electoral politics took not only to the streets but to the farm fields. Agriculture, like nearly everything else, had become an industry since World War II. Crop yields had been boosted by chemical fertilizers, hybrid seeds, insecticides, and herbicides, along with mechanical equipment of ever-increasing size and power. Chickens and turkeys were no longer raised in farmyards but in steel barns filled with permanent cages and automated systems for feeding and watering. Hogs and cattle were fattened by the thousands in feed lots, and dairy cows in the hundreds were milked by machine. A new word—"agribusiness"—referred to the large companies that not only supplied the input but handled the storage and worldwide marketing of the commodities produced.

All of this called for large-scale business operations and capital investment. Family farming as a way of life was ending, and through the 1960s and '70s the watchword in farm country was "get big or get out." Many farmers got out. A period of high commodity prices in the early 1970s drove up the value of land, and those who opted to "get big" mortgaged their farms to finance expansion. When prices crashed in the late seventies they faced a wave of foreclosures. By 1980 the size of farms in Minnesota's part of the corn belt had nearly doubled since 1950, and the number of people working on all Minnesota farms had fallen by nearly half.

As the Reagan era opened, farm protest still existed in Minnesota, but compared with earlier times the voice of farmers was feeble. That of the giant agribusiness corporations was louder, and they spoke with money. The National Farm Organization (NFO), founded in Iowa in 1955, tried to repeat the holding actions of the Farmers' Holiday Association, but like its predecessor it had little success. "Tractorcades" that rolled through the streets of Washington and St. Paul in the late 1970s and early 1980s to demand price supports and a moratorium on farm foreclosures produced great photo ops but made no impression on the Republican administration in either capitol.

One opportunity remaining to small-scale farmers was the emerging organic market, in part created by the new food co-ops. Those who had gone to the country in search of an alternative lifestyle were quick to seize it. By the early 1970s they had joined together in an Organic Growers and Buyers Association, formed for mutual support in marketing and for defense against false claims of organic production. By the

1980s more traditional small farmers were recognizing the damage to Minnesota's soil and water created by industrial agriculture. Organizations like the Land Stewardship Project, the Minnesota Food Association, and the Organic Consumers Association joined forces with the health-food co-ops to protest environmental devastation and to increase the demand for products of sustainable farming.

In the 1990s biochemical and pharmaceutical firms like Monsanto joined the ranks of agribusiness corporations. Genetic engineering became an issue, along with the routine use of antibiotics in raising animals and dubious experiments like bovine growth hormone, which was legally introduced in 1993. Alarm for human health was thus added to concern for the land. Slowly the state began to realize that organics, although still a very small proportion of Minnesota agriculture, had become its fastest-growing sector.

Energy was another disturbing issue among the state's farmers and rural communities, closely related to the use of oil in chemical fertilizers and as fuel for heavy farm machinery. U.S. dependence on foreign oil was brought home to the country by an acute shortage in the mid-1970s. Minnesota has few energy sources of any kind except wind, and even before the oil crisis the state's growing metro region was looking westward toward the large deposits of low-grade coal in the Dakotas and Wyoming. Shipping this coal to Minnesota had been too expensive in the past, but new technology made it possible to send power cheaply from electric generating plants in central North Dakota to the Twin Cities.

Plans for a giant power line were far along before farmers whose land it would cross in central Minnesota even heard about it. Then there was a storm of protest. No one wanted the huge towers in their fields, and there were many unanswered questions about the effects on animals and people of the new direct-current transmission. Surveyors for the line were stopped by landowners in Minnesota's conservative heartland. Local governments in Grant, Pope, and Stearns counties tried to block it by refusing permits, but the state overruled them. When construction crews arrived, they were met by crowds of protesters who had to be driven from their own fields by squads of state police. Many of them were women. According to Alice Tripp, one of the leaders,

> We discovered that the state government and even the courts operated in favor of established business. Keeping the wheels turning—no matter what the consequences to individuals—is important to our legal system. In St. Paul and in Washington, the pressure of the business establishment has more influence than the voice of the people. So when we resisted and opposed first the utilities then the law, we were not ashamed. There were over one hundred arrests in the winter of 1978—people who had never broken even traffic laws. People who had paid their taxes and their bills all their lives, who felt they had used every legal channel and had received no help from their own government, were defying the court's injunctions.

Even after the towers were up, resistance continued. "Bolt weevils" attacked them at night, and some came crashing down. Using the old name Farmer Labor Association, Tripp ran for governor against Perpich and received 100,000 votes in the primary election of 1978. Another of the protest organizers, a young professor from Carleton College, published a book three years later under the title *Powerline: The First Battle of America's Energy War*. His name was Paul Wellstone.

*   *   *

On the labor side of the old alliance, the story was much the same. As in the rest of the country, union membership had declined, but unions had made little effort to enroll women and minorities. The only large gains had been in the organizing of teachers and government workers. On the Iron Range foreign competition had ended the taconite boom and times were lean again. In 1976–77 the longest steelworkers' strike on record ended after 138 days with little to show for it. A strike of a wholly different kind in Willmar was ignored by the state's labor leaders. There, eight women employed by the Citizens National Bank quit work and started picketing in 1977 when they were told that it was useless to apply for promotion because "We're not all equal, you know." The effort lasted two years, and none of them was rehired. National attention, however, was called to the blatant discrimination against women in white collar and professional jobs.

Many national unions seemed willing to accept the role of junior partners to American industry. That attitude was important in Minnesota's fiercest labor battle of the late twentieth century. The conflict occurred at the Hormel plant in Austin, which had also been the scene of a crucial struggle in 1933. In the years between, Hormel had become a national symbol of enlightened labor policy.

Beginning in 1982, when Hormel opened a new plant financed in part by the savings of its workers, Local P-9 of the United Food and Commercial Workers (UFCW) agreed to a long series of concessions, including wage cuts and speedups. But in the summer of 1985, faced with yet more demands from a company that was among the most profitable in Minnesota, the workers voted to strike. Austin is largely a company town, and the conflict soon involved a broad slice of the community, including a support group for the strikers that numbered

The "Willmar 8" picketed the Citizens National Bank of Willmar through bitter winter weather.

more than five hundred family members and friends. Local farmers, peace activists, women's groups, and members of Jesse Jackson's Rainbow Coalition also gave help. Again one of the active strike supporters was Paul Wellstone, the firebrand from Northfield.

Ordinary members of other packinghouse locals around the country supported P-9, but the officers of the international UFCW opposed both the strike and the tactics used, which included putting pressure on the First Bank System, Hormel's principal creditor. Eventually, the courts issued an injunction under the Taft-Hartley Act to prevent a "secondary boycott" against the bank, and the international union withheld funds and evicted Local P-9 from its own strike headquarters in Austin. Finally, in January 1986, Hormel reopened the plant with

nonunion workers, and DFL governor Rudy Perpich, claiming
that violence was threatened, sent National Guard troops to
prevent picketing. Thus the strike was crushed by those who
were thought to be friends of labor.

Like farmers and workers, peace activists were driven to the
streets and to civil disobedience in the 1980s. The unpopular
draft law that had sent many young men to Canada during the
Vietnam War had expired in 1973, but in 1980 Congress again
required them to register with Selective Service. In Minnesota
as elsewhere, hundreds refused. As one Macalester College
student who resisted said, "Registration is being used as more
than a mechanism for a draft. It is also fulfilling a purpose
of subservience to a military establishment through force. It's
making young men say, 'I'm in agreement with your purpose,'
and giving the decision-making power then to the military
concerning their own lives."

President Reagan also called for a whole new generation
of short-range nuclear missiles in a state of hair-trigger alert
to be deployed in the NATO nations of Europe. This brought
a wave of fear and opposition in Europe and aroused an energetic but short-lived Nuclear Freeze movement in the United
States. A striking feature of this new wave of antiwar protests
was the leadership of women. A worldwide symbol of this
emerged in Britain when women established a center for resistance near an RAF base at Greenham Common in Berkshire.
At this women's peace camp, tens of thousands marched and
demonstrated between 1981 and 1991. American women responded by surrounding the Pentagon with a chain of ribbons
and peace symbols in 1981 and establishing peace camps of
their own in the years that followed.

A lasting mark of the new wave in Minnesota was the founding in 1981 of Women Against Military Madness (WAMM). It was followed in 1983 by a short-lived women's peace camp on public land in front of the Sperry Company headquarters in St. Paul. The same year saw a major demonstration by the longstanding Honeywell Project when more than five hundred people were arrested around the Minneapolis headquarters of the state's largest arms manufacturer. After 1990, when Honeywell formed a subsidiary named Alliant Techsystems to handle its military contracts, the protests continued under the name AlliantACTION. The person most closely associated with them has been perennial militant Marv Davidov.

Fifty years of cold war came to an end in the late 1980s when Soviet premier Mikhail Gorbachev relaxed the tight fist of military dictatorship and freed the countries of Eastern Europe from Soviet control. This was followed shortly by the breaking up of the Soviet Union. Hopes for a peaceful world were immediately dashed, however, by the First Gulf War, started when the United States attacked Iraq in response to the invasion of Kuwait by Iraqi forces in 1990.

14. ECOPOLITICS AND NEW PARTIES

ON AUGUST 10–12, 1984, A GROUP OF SIXTY-TWO SPOKES-people for cultural and environmental change gathered on the campus of Macalester College in St. Paul. The national conference was inspired by news from Europe and particularly by the publication of the book *Green Politics: The Global Promise,* by Charlene Spretnak and Fritjof Capra. Those invited had little grounding in practical politics. They represented movements ranging from bioregionalism to social ecology, to community organizing, to futurism, to ecofeminism. Notably missing were voices from the radical left, and as described by Mark Satin, the editor of *New Options* newsletter, the gathering had a distinctly New Age flavor: "For two days and nights they sat in a circle trying hard to get to know and trust one another and reach some semblance of agreement. It wasn't easy . . . The meeting began with an 'imaging exercise.' People self-selected into groups of three, got comfortable on the carpet or sofas, and were asked to silently imagine what life in a future 'Green Society' could be like."

Nevertheless, it was politics that had brought them together. By 1980 nearly every European country had a small Green Party, and others were scattered around the globe. They had sprung from growing fears for the planetary environment and were loosely defined by agreement to four principles: grassroots democracy, social and economic justice, ecological wisdom, and nonviolence. In 1983 German voters had startled the world by sending twenty-eight Greens to the Bundestag. After traveling in Europe and talking with leaders of the movement, Spretnak and Capra were urging Americans to join it.

Europe's experience was little help. Those meeting in Minnesota faced a sprawling country with multiple political units, an entrenched two-party system, and a variety of militant identity groups. In less than three days, however, they managed to reach agreement on ten "key values," which included the four international principles plus six more, listed at various times as community-based economics, decentralization, feminism, respect for diversity, personal and global responsibility, and future focus. The conferees honored decentralization by establishing no national organization but only a clearinghouse for communication among separate Green groups around the country. The clearinghouse remained in St. Paul for a year, then was moved to Kansas City.

During its first decade the Upper Midwest Green movement was closely linked with Native Americans in both Minnesota and Wisconsin. Two of the early local groups—the Lake Superior Greens and the St. Croix Valley Greens—formed on bioregional lines and straddled the border of the two states. Their members were quickly swept up in the cause of off-reservation hunting and fishing rights. A court decision had triggered the issue in 1983 when it affirmed Chippewa (Ojibwe) tribal rights to traditional hunting and fishing, including the use of spears, throughout northern Wisconsin. Those rights had been allowed in nineteenth-century U.S. treaties but had been forbidden by states for years. The decision was appealed, and after a trip through the courts it was reaffirmed in 1987.

Walter Bresette, an Ojibwe artist, journalist, and active Green from the Red Cliff Reservation in northern Wisconsin, took the lead in forming the Upper Great Lakes Green Network in 1987. As Ojibwe people prepared to exercise their restored rights, they were fiercely opposed by local white sportsmen's groups. At Bresette's urging, Greens and others sympathetic to Indian rights gathered at boat landings where threatening white crowds confronted Indian fishermen. Tension was high for four seasons, but the tribe allowed no overfishing, and the presence of organized witnesses helped prevent serious violence.

Lurking behind spearfishing was the more fundamental issue of copper, nickel, and uranium mining in northern Wisconsin. "If the Chippewa model succeeds," wrote Bresette, "Native rights, will be the last bastion of environmental and economic stability on the continent." The tie of indigenous people with saving the earth, and by extension with the Green movement, was championed also by Winona LaDuke, from the White Earth Reservation in Minnesota, who in 1995 joined Bresette in advocating a "Seventh Generation Amendment" to the U.S. Constitution: "The right of the people to use and enjoy air, water, sunlight, and other renewable resources determined by Congress to be common property, shall not be impaired, nor shall such use impair their availability for future generations."

Twin Cities Greens had been meeting since 1986 and had drawn together a handful of smaller groups along the state's eastern border into a Minnesota Green Confederation. Beginning in the 1990s their attention became focused on the struggle over nuclear power. The Prairie Island plant, owned by Northern States Power Company (NSP), was running out of storage space for its high-level radioactive wastes, and the company asked permission from the state to use aboveground casks. Environmentalists and Native Americans pointed out that the site of such storage would be on the flood plain of the Mississippi River and only a few hundred yards from a Dakota Indian community. For nearly four years Greens led a coalition of environmental groups, churches, and some tribal members in opposition to the measure. In 1994, behind closed doors, legislators appointed to a conference committee agreed to a limited number of "temporary" casks.

Nationally, Greens were divided among those who wanted to continue as a bioregional protest movement and those who wanted to be a functioning political party. In 1991 a Green Party Organizing Committee broke away from what had become the Greens/Green Party USA and encouraged the forming of state-based green parties oriented toward electoral politics. A national meeting of the G/GPUSA held in Minneapolis in 1992 was the last such gathering for several years, as unaffiliated parties became active in Alaska, Hawaii, and a number of western states. Wisconsin had organized a state party in 1988, and Minnesota Greens, faced with declining membership, followed the trend in 1994. Walt Bresette gave the keynote address at the Minnesota party's organizing convention.

With the approach of the presidential election in 1996, a provisional Association of State Green Parties endorsed consumer advocate Ralph Nader for president. He chose Minnesota's Winona LaDuke as his running mate. As in most other states, the main struggle in Minnesota was to collect enough

signatures on petitions to place the party's candidates on
the ballot. Greens succeeded in doing this in 1996 and again
in 1998 when Ken Pentel and Susan Jasper, an Anishinabe
(Ojibwe), ran for governor and lieutenant governor.

Another attempt at third-party progressive politics had appeared in 1992. The Twin Cities Area New Party (later called
Progressive Minnesota and now merged in Take Action) was
linked with a broader movement that was inspired by Jesse
Jackson's Rainbow Coalition, formed in 1984 when Jackson
campaigned for the Democratic presidential nomination. Although the New Party and its members claimed to be independent, it was widely regarded by outsiders as a Democratic
Party faction. Its immediate goal was elimination of the fusion laws by which most states, including Minnesota, forbade
a candidate to be identified with more than one party on an
election ballot. This was only one of many legal barriers that
had been raised quietly against third parties in the course of
the twentieth century.

In 1997, when the U.S. Supreme Court sustained Minnesota's fusion law, the New Party faded fast, and after a few local
campaigns it became inactive. By then, however, the swelling
discontent that had produced it had found at least one ringing voice within the DFL itself. Left-leaning activists, angry
at Perpich and his pro-business policies, rallied around Paul
Wellstone, whose boundless energy and impassioned speaking style drew widespread attention. Wellstone chaired Jackson's Minnesota effort in 1988, and in 1990 he received DFL
endorsement in what was widely thought to be a hopeless race
for the U.S. Senate.

The Republican incumbent, Rudy Boschwitz, had been the
first Jew elected to a statewide office in Minnesota. He was

also a millionaire businessman whose fund-raising talent and folksy style seemed unbeatable. Added to his resources was his reputation in the Senate as a powerful spokesman for the interests of Israel.

In a campaign that became legendary, Wellstone used humor and his own underdog status, touring the state in a green-painted school bus and speaking to audiences wherever he could find them. The Wellstone bus seemed to be running low on gas the week before election day, but then Boschwitz and his team took a wrong turn. In a letter to a number of leading Minnesota Jews, they said bluntly that Wellstone, who was also Jewish, "had no connection whatsoever with the Jewish community or our communal life." The letter pointed to the fact that Wellstone's wife, Sheila, was a Christian and that their children had been raised outside the Jewish faith. The religious attack on Wellstone's family stirred anger among many voters, both Jewish and Christian. The anger was enough to give Wellstone a narrow victory at the polls.

The new senator's populist style and outspoken opposition to the First Gulf War made for a prickly start in the closed club of the U.S. Senate, but in time his integrity won respect. As he said, he represented "the democratic wing of the Democratic Party," and therefore he was shunned by the party's leadership. Nevertheless, his determination "to drive big money out of politics and drive people in" won him reelection by Minnesotans in 1996.

During the 1990s yet another minor party appeared in Minnesota. Although it was hardly progressive, it served as a focus for those protesting the growing radicalism of Republican rightists. In 1992 a maverick Texas billionaire named Ross Perot ran for president against the candidates of the two ma-

jor parties and received nearly 20 percent of the country's
popular vote. In Minnesota he received 24 percent. His most
prominent position was opposition to the North American
Free Trade Agreement (NAFTA), which was widely opposed
also by labor unions. His inclusion in the nationally televised
presidential debates was credited with boosting his support,
and the major parties arranged to prevent that from ever hap-
pening again.

Perot backers in Minnesota organized as the Independence
Party of Minnesota (IPM) and nominated Dean Barkley for a
seat in Congress. While conservative on fiscal issues, Barkley
and his party remained liberal on social questions. His stated
position on abortion carried a libertarian touch: "Any government that has the power to prevent a woman from having an
abortion also has the power to require one. I do not want to
give this power to the Federal Government."

When Perot organized a national Reform Party in prepa-
ration for running again in 1996, the IPM affiliated with it
and became the Reform Party of Minnesota. Two years later
it nominated for governor a former champion wrestler and
talk-show host whose professional name was Jesse Ventura.
He had served as mayor of the suburb of Brooklyn Park and
had become identified with the affluent younger generation
in the communities circling the Twin Cities. To the surprise
of the entire country, Ventura was elected in an evenly split
three-way race.

The victory of Jesse ("The Body") Ventura testified to the
growing influence of celebrity and entertainment in American
politics and also to the growing population and power of the
suburbs. Another factor may have been the state's same-day
registration law. There is evidence that many of his supporters were last-minute voters. His campaign had cost less than

a million dollars in a time when campaign funds in the tens of millions were commonplace, and he made a public appeal for money to fund his flamboyant inaugural ball.

Although Ventura showed both shrewdness and moderation in running the state, he had little interest in building the party that had supported him, and he put forth no clear political aims. He declined to try for a second term. By the year 2000 Perot also had lost interest in the Reform Party, and its leadership had fallen to the far-rightist commentator Pat Buchanan. At that point the Minnesota party withdrew and returned to its original name of Independence Party and its middle-of-the-road conservatism.

The Minnesota Green Party had held passionately to its environmental and social ideology and had worked to build a platform that would speak to immediate issues and attract candidates for local and state offices. It was handicapped by refusing on principle to accept money from any corporate source, including liberal political action committees, and it was steadily ignored by the mainstream media. The election of 2000 brought an abrupt change, however.

As in 1996 Ralph Nader and Winona LaDuke were national candidates. Although excluded from the presidential debates, Nader drew unexpected support in the face of a slowing economy and a looming environmental crisis. Ten thousand Minnesotans cheered him at a rally in Minneapolis, and he received more than 5 percent of the state's vote. In spite of Nader's popularity, the DFL carried the state for Democrat Al Gore, but charges of "spoiler" became common political currency.

The vote level for the Greens, however, gave them major party status in Minnesota until the next presidential election, which meant that they had a ballot line without petitioning and were eligible for modest state campaign funding. In the governor's race of 2002, the team of Ken Pentel, nominated for governor, and Rhoda Gilman, for lieutenant governor, qualified for matching state funds, and for the first time the Green Party was able to support a truly statewide campaign with a full slate of candidates. None, however, reached the crucial 5 percent vote that would have preserved the party's status and ballot line.

Divisions in the Green Party were highlighted by a struggle over supporting a candidate to oppose Paul Wellstone, who, contrary to a previous pledge, ran for a third term in the Senate. A sizeable minority of Greens opposed mounting a challenge to him. The initial endorsement of Ed McGaa, a Lakota from the Pine Ridge Reservation, as the party's candidate for U.S. Senate proved a disaster when it became clear that he did not uphold Green Party values and campaigned largely on his long career with the U.S. Marines. As a major party the Greens participated in the primary election that year, and McGaa was replaced by Ray Tricomo, a little-known teacher and environmentalist.

For the state as a whole, 2002 was a historic election year, with four legally recognized major parties contending for state offices. Governor Ventura was replaced on the Independence Party's ticket by Tim Penny, a former DFL congressman from southern Minnesota; the DFL slate was headed by Roger Moe, and the Republican by Tim Pawlenty. The hardest-fought race, however, was for U.S. senator. Paul Wellstone was opposed by Norm Coleman, mayor of St. Paul and a rightist Democrat-turned-Republican. A week before election day, with the result too close to call, Wellstone, his wife Sheila, their daughter, and several campaign aides all died in a plane crash near Eveleth.

The tragedy, for which no specific cause was ever found, left Minnesota shaken and the DFL without a senatorial candidate. Despite the effort of elder statesman Walter Mondale, who stood in during the final week, the state elected Republicans as both governor and senator by narrow pluralities.

CONCLUSION: STAND UP!

THE ELECTION OF 2000 HAD SEATED GEORGE W. BUSH IN the White House by decree of the U.S. Supreme Court after he had received a still doubtful majority of electoral votes and had lost the nation's popular vote to Democrat Al Gore. Questions thus raised about the fairness of the electoral college system and the honesty of the ballot box were reinforced by events in Ohio during the close election of 2004 and by the vast amounts of private money continually poured into campaigning and lobbying.

The evenly balanced voting pattern in Minnesota has acted as a magnet for millions of dollars that have poisoned elections. In 2005 the Center for Public Integrity ranked it fourth among states in the amount of special interest money spent. A later demonstration was the 2008 race for U.S. Senate. After record-breaking expenditures on both sides, DFL television personality Al Franken beat incumbent Republican Norm Coleman by 314 votes. The close outcome was contested through seven months of wrangling and court action during which an additional twenty-one million dollars was spent. Symbolic of the state's sharp polarization is its representation by Congress members at opposite ends of the political spectrum: Michele Bachmann, a nationally recognized voice for the Christian right and the Tea Party movement, and Keith Ellison, the only Muslim in Congress and a left-leaning member of the Black caucus.

To discouragement with the electoral process was added fear and a sense of futility in protesting on the streets. The nationwide hysteria following the events of September 11, 2001, was reminiscent of that which accompanied World War I. It threw a dark question mark over the right to assemble and to plan or engage in civil disobedience, and the passage of both national and state Patriot Acts gave law enforcement authorities a broad new array of tools to use against protesters. Historic worldwide peace demonstrations held before the U.S. invasion of Iraq in March 2003 were downplayed or ignored by the country's major news organizations, as was local opposition to the war. The overriding of international law and of constitutional protections for the freedom and privacy of U.S. citizens went unchallenged in Congress.

Minnesota's long tradition of contentious protest proved stubborn, however. Antiwar demonstrations continued, led by organizations like WAMM and AlliantACTION, while religious groups like the Quakers and local members of Pax Christi held regular peace vigils. Those were countered by rallies and demonstrations that addressed social issues of the religious right like gay marriage and abortion and mainly converged at the state capitol.

Both the Green and Independence parties maintained an active presence. The Greens continued to build strength at the local level, where offices that were nominally nonpartisan

made ballot access easier. They elected several city council
members in Minneapolis and ran strong mayoral campaigns
in both Minneapolis and St. Paul. In these contests candidates
known to be Republican often found themselves in third place,
and the Greens threatened to become the main alternative to
the ruling DFL among city voters. In 2006 the Green Party
lost its state ballot line, yet its members performed the historic feat of collecting more than seventeen thousand signatures
in three weeks and thus running a full slate of state candidates, despite being legally a minor party. The Independence
Party, more active in state elections and still holding major
party status, acquired two incumbent state senators from districts outside the Twin Cities. Both had felt forced to transfer
allegiance from the increasingly extremist Republican Party.

In 2008 the DFL mayors of St. Paul and Minneapolis united in a successful bid to host the Republican National Convention. In spite of high hopes, it brought little advantage to
the business of either city and disaster to their reputation for
freedom and civil liberty. Although local authorities promised
unchecked expression and protection for peaceful demonstrators, the scene changed abruptly when federal security forces
swept into St. Paul with ranks of police imported from elsewhere and new restrictions on access to the city and the convention center. Invasions of property and detentions before
the convention were followed at the end by some eight hundred arrests amid clouds of pepper spray and Taser fire. Journalists not "embedded" with the police were targeted for attack. Among the twenty-two people eventually taken to court
for various offenses were the "RNC 8": eight young people
who proudly claimed to be anarchists planning nonviolent
civil disobedience. The initial charges against them, of felony
conspiracy to commit riot "in furtherance of terrorism," were

During the 2008 Republican National Convention, police arrested young concert-goers in a St. Paul park.

subsequently dismissed or reduced to gross misdemeanors. The chilling threat to protest remains.

At the end of 2010, the continued influence of the Independence Party had for the fourth time produced a close election in which the winner, this time DFL governor Mark Dayton, represents a minority of Minnesotans. This has led to renewed calls for a change in the electoral system to ranked choice (also known as instant runoff) voting, which has already been adopted by both Minneapolis and St. Paul. For the first time since 1913, the Republican Party officially controls both houses of the Minnesota legislature, although de facto control existed through most of the sixty years in which the legislature was nominally nonpartisan. Further uncertainty looms ahead with the redrawing of the state's electoral districts as a result of the 2010 U.S. census.

* * *

In just over 150 years since 1858, the millions of hands that were reaching out for acres have claimed Minnesota's woods and prairies and turned them into townships, sections, and fenced fields. The transformation demanded nearly two generations of exhausted lives and backbreaking labor, but many of the new Minnesotans had fled starvation and oppression in Europe, and the land promised them freedom, dignity, and a future for their children. The story they told themselves was a tale of bringing the light of civilization to a dark and untamed wilderness and making it bloom with "sunlight and music, and gladsome flower."

Civilization did its work in those 150 years. Tons of grain, flour, and meat have been shipped from the state to feed a hungry world. Minnesota lumber has built towns and farms across the treeless plains, and its iron ore has supplied steel for cities and for two world wars. It is at the center of a network of railroads and highways and is connected by oceangoing ships and steel barges with both the Atlantic Ocean and the Gulf of Mexico. Even more fundamental may be the new web of communication that links it by computer with every corner of the globe. More than five million people from Europe, Asia, and Africa now call the state home, and its population is more diverse than ever before.

But there have been costs. The native people living on the land were dispossessed and driven out or confined to pockets of poverty called reservations, with their culture and sacred places devastated and their beliefs condemned. The tall pine forests that covered half the state are gone. So is the rich iron ore. Most of the ten thousand lakes and once-clear streams are polluted with silt, sewage, or chemical fallout from the air. Much of the fertile prairie topsoil has been washed down the Mississippi, where it adds to a spreading dead zone in the

Gulf of Mexico. The level of groundwater has been lowered by draining natural wetlands to create even more acres for crops at the expense of wildlife habitat and overflow basins for excess rainfall. Great wealth came from this process of stripping the land, but it did not benefit all equally. Abuse of resources that are held in common and needed by all, plus the unrelenting drive for economic growth, are still leading to destruction and to accumulation of more wealth in the hands of a few.

The years have also seen a perpetual struggle to preserve the democracy and equality without which freedom cannot exist. Minnesota's maverick record of protest politics can be traced to the hopes of its immigrants and to the literacy and hunger for education that came along with them. From its earliest days the state had an exceptional number of local newspapers in many languages. Its early leaders secured from the U.S. government twice the area of public land normally granted for schools, and its first territorial legislature enacted an unusually strong common school law. Two years later visionary legislators chartered a university. The demand for both teachers and preachers led to the early opening of small colleges to train them. Interest in community and in government followed naturally. As outlined here, demands that the public good take priority over private gain have been heard from all corners of the state—from the high coteau of southwestern Minnesota and the wheat fields of the Red River Valley to the ore docks of Duluth and the mills of Minneapolis.

As a result, Minnesota has been relatively prosperous, and until recently it has had fine public services, outstanding schools and health care, and workers eager and able to handle new technology. By the mid-twentieth century, its tax structure was the fairest in the nation, and Minnesota was a leader among the states in its number of nonprofit corporations and philanthropies. In spite of a slow start and fierce opposition from ethnic and special interests, Minnesota's women have gained important roles in government, the courts, and business, although their position is still far from equal. Significant natural areas have been saved for parks, and wilderness preserves have been guarded. Not for nothing has Minnesota grown large in national influence and been called "a state that works." Yet none of this was achieved without repeated waves of demand at the ballot box, in workplaces, and on the streets.

Looking to the future, Minnesota, like the rest of the nation and the world, faces unprecedented threats. Since the 1940s the United States has never really ceased being at war. It has become a militarized country and the world's largest merchant of advanced weaponry. As Minnesota's Eugene McCarthy pointed out, war has become our chief instrument of policy whether against other nations or our own people—as seen today in the war on drugs and the appalling numbers of people we send to prison.

But war is only one of the threats. We now see the dark side of industrial civilization—in climate change, the passing of cheap oil, extinction of species, poisonous pollution, and shortages of fresh water. As environmentalists and advocates of an alternative lifestyle have been saying for fifty years, survival of human society calls for enormous changes on both a global and a local level. In facing the need for change, Minnesota's most precious asset will be its tradition of uniting against injustice and against the concentrated power of money and corporations. It has bred a sense of community, and the persistent call for social justice and human rights harmonizes fundamentally with the undercurrent of religious and spiritual ethics that has helped shape the state.

SOURCES AND FURTHER READING

MUCH OF THE STORY ON WHICH THIS BOOK IS BASED CAN be found in general histories and collections. Some of these include: Anne J. Aby, ed., *The North Star State: A Minnesota History Reader* (2002); Rhoda R. Gilman, *The Story of Minnesota's Past* (1989); Stephen E. Graubard, ed., *Minnesota, Real and Imagined* (2000); Steven J. Keillor, *Shaping Minnesota's Identity* (2008); William E. Lass, *Minnesota: A History* (2nd edition, 1998); Daniel J. Elazar, Virginia Gray, and Wyman Spano, *Minnesota Politics and Government* (1999).

An indispensable source for the nineteenth and early twentieth centuries is William W. Folwell's *A History of Minnesota*. Although published in the 1920s and reflecting the attitudes and perspectives of an earlier time, Folwell's work remains a remarkably objective, scholarly, and readable account of the years 1849–1920, through which the author himself lived and played an active role. For the twentieth century an especially valuable source is Clifford E. Clark Jr., ed., *Minnesota in a Century of Change: The State and Its People Since 1900* (1989).

Grouped below by chapter are works that discuss particular periods. The list makes no attempt at completeness and is simply a starting point for further reading.

CHAPTER 1

Rhoda R. Gilman, *Henry Hastings Sibley: Divided Heart* (2004)

Mary Lethert Wingerd, *North Country: The Making of Minnesota* (2010)

"The Acres and the Hands" is from the *Daily Minnesotian* (St. Paul), December 18, 1860; the resolutions of the Military Reserve Claim Association are in the manuscripts collection of the Minnesota Historical Society.

CHAPTER 2

William Anderson, *A History of the Constitution of Minnesota* (1921)

William D. Green, *A Peculiar Imbalance: The Fall and Rise of Racial Equality in Early Minnesota* (2007)

"The Abolition Wagon" is from the *Chatfield Democrat*, May 24, 1862; Perkins's words, along with those of many others, can be found in *Debates and Proceedings of the Constitutional Convention for the Territory of Minnesota;* Donnelly's address to immigrants is in the *Daily Minnesotian*, June 15, 1859.

CHAPTER 3

Annette Atkins, *Harvest of Grief: Grasshopper Plagues and Public Assistance in Minnesota, 1873–78* (1984)

Solon J. Buck, *The Granger Movement* (1913)

Gilman, *Henry Hastings Sibley*

Martin Ridge, *Ignatius Donnelly: Portrait of a Politician* (1962)

The letters from farmers are in the Minnesota Governors' Archives; Donnelly's statements to Grangers are from *Facts for the Granges* (1873), copy in the Minnesota Historical Society library. The greenback verses and Donnelly's "brass kettle" speech are from the *Anti-Monopolist*, October 17 and October 31, 1878.

CHAPTER 4

Elizabeth Faue, *Writing the Wrongs: Eva Valesh and the Rise of Labor Journalism* (2002)

John D. Hicks, *The Populist Revolt: A History of the Farmers' Alliance and the People's Party* (1931)

Ridge, *Ignatius Donnelly*

The Alliance resolutions of 1886 are in *Minnesota State Farmers' Alliance, Declaration of Rights*, copy in the Minnesota Historical Society library. Donnelly's preamble to the Populist Party platform of 1892 has been reprinted many times; the complete document is in Hicks's *Populist Revolt*.

CHAPTER 5

Richard Hudelson and Carl Ross, *By the Ore Docks: A Working People's History of Duluth* (2006)

Marvin G. Lamppa, *Minnesota's Iron Country: Rich Ore, Rich Lives* (2004)

Albro Martin, *James J. Hill and the Opening of the Northwest* (1976)

William Millikan, *A Union Against Unions: The Minneapolis Citizens Alliance and Its Fight Against Organized Labor, 1903–1947* (2001)

Carl Ross, *The Finn Factor in American Labor, Culture and Society* (1977)

Nick Salvatore, *Eugene V. Debs, Citizen and Socialist* (1982)

The Wobbly verses, written to the tune of "It's a Long Road

to Tipperary," are said to have appeared first in the IWW publication *Solidarity*, August 5, 1916. The full version can be found in *Minnesota History* 41.2 (1968): 94.

CHAPTER 6

Heidi Bauer, ed., *The Privilege for Which We Struggled: Leaders of the Woman Suffrage Movement in Minnesota* (1999)

Carl H. Chrislock, *The Progressive Era in Minnesota, 1899–1918* (1971)

Martin, *James J. Hill*

The words of Cushman K. Davis are from a lecture delivered to the Minnesota Bar Association in 1895; they are reprinted in Theodore C. Blegen and Philip D. Jordan, eds., *With Various Voices: Readings of North Star Life*. The quotation from Clara Ueland is from a pamphlet entitled *The Advantages of Equal Suffrage* (1914); a copy is in the Minnesota Historical Society's collections. The passage about the influence of Minnesota's special interests was written by Lynn Haines and published in *LaFollette's Weekly Magazine* for October 1910.

CHAPTER 7

Carl H. Chrislock, *Watchdog of Loyalty: The Minnesota Commission of Public Safety During World War I* (1991)

Hudelson and Ross, *By the Ore Docks*

Bruce L. Larson, *Lindbergh of Minnesota: A Political Biography* (1973)

Millikan, *A Union Against Unions*

Robert L. Morlan, *Political Prairie Fire: The Nonpartisan League, 1915–1922* (1955)

The two letters to Nelson are in the Knute Nelson Papers in the Minnesota Historical Society; the first was written by William Huper. The press release from the Public Safety Commission, dated January 19, 1918, is in the Arthur LeSueur Papers in the Minnesota Historical Society.

CHAPTER 8

Millard L. Gieske, *Minnesota Farmer-Laborism: The Third-Party Alternative* (1979)

George H. Mayer, *The Political Career of Floyd B. Olson* (1951)

Ross, *The Finn Factor*

Barbara Stuhler, *Ten Men of Minnesota and American Foreign Policy* (1973)

The quotations from John Bosch are from an oral history interview in the collection of the Southwest Minnesota Historical Center. Excerpts were published in *Minnesota History* 44.8 (1975): 304–8.

CHAPTER 9

Elizabeth Faue, *Community of Suffering and Struggle: Women, Men, and the Labor Movement in Minneapolis, 1915–1945* (1991)

Gieske, *Minnesota Farmer-Laborism*

Lamppa, *Minnesota's Iron Country*

Mayer, *Floyd B. Olson*

Millikan, *A Union Against Unions*

Ross, *The Finn Factor*

Olson's words to the Farmer-Labor convention of 1934 have been quoted often; they can be found in Mayer, *Floyd B. Olson.*

CHAPTER 10

Jennifer A. Delton, *Making Minnesota Liberal: Civil Rights and the Transformation of the Democratic Party* (2002)

Gieske, *Minnesota Farmer-Laborism*

John Earl Haynes, *Dubious Alliance: The Making of Minnesota's DFL Party* (1984)

Hudelson and Ross, *By the Ore Docks*

Steven J. Keillor, *Hjalmar Petersen of Minnesota: The Politics of Provincial Independence* (1987)

Robert Latz, *Jews in Minnesota Politics* (2007)

James M. Shields, *Mr. Progressive: A Biography of Elmer Austin Benson* (1971)

Carl Solberg, *Hubert Humphrey: A Biography* (1984)

Stuhler, *Ten Men of Minnesota*

Benson's letter appears in Shields, *Mr. Progressive*. The two quotations from Humphrey are in Solberg, *Hubert Humphrey*.

CHAPTER 11

Delton, *Making Minnesota Liberal*

Rhoda R. Gilman, ed., *Ringing in the Wilderness: Selections from the* North Country Anvil (1996)

Latz, *Jews in Minnesota Politics*

Solberg, *Hubert Humphrey*

Billie Young and Nancy Ankenny, *Minnesota Women in Politics: Stories of the Journey* (2000)

McCarthy's speech is reprinted in Eugene J. McCarthy, *The Year of the People* (1969).

CHAPTER 12

Gilman, *Ringing in the Wilderness*

Craig Cox, *Storefront Revolution: Food Co-ops and the Counterculture* (1994)

The quotations from Jack Miller and from the member of the Georgetown commune are in Gilman, ed., *Ringing in the Wilderness*. The Port Huron Statement in its entire length is available on the Internet; see also Tom Hayden, *The Port Huron Statement: The Visionary Call of the 1960s Revolution* (2005).

CHAPTER 13

Bill Lofy, *Paul Wellstone: The Life of a Passionate Progressive* (2005)

Peter Rachleff, *Hard-Pressed in the Heartland: The Hormel Strike and the Future of the Labor Movement* (1993)

Neala J. Schleuning, *Women, Community, and the Hormel Strike of 1985–86* (1994)

Paul Wellstone and Berry M. Casper, *Powerline: The First Battle of America's Energy War* (1981)

The words of Alice Tripp are from her essay in Gilman, ed., *Ringing in the Wilderness;* those of Macalester College student Phillip Beisswenger are quoted in the essay by Mordecai Specktor, also in *Ringing in the Wilderness.*

CHAPTER 14

Greta Gaard, *Ecological Politics: Ecofeminists and the Greens* (1998)

Latz, *Jews in Minnesota Politics*

John Rensenbrink, *The Greens and the Politics of Transformation* (1992)

Rick Whaley with Walter Bresette, *Walleye Warriors: An Effective Alliance Against Racism and for the Earth* (1994)

The account of the first U.S. Green convention by Mark Satin was quoted in the *North Country Anvil* 48 (Summer-Fall, 1984). The quotation from Dean Barkley is from an interview conducted in 2008. See www.ontheissues.org.

INDEX